DOLLY CONNELLY, conservationist and outdoor enthusiast, began her career as a newspaperwoman. She then progressed to news magazines and, finally, to magazines of all types, for which she has written and photographed hundreds of articles on diverse subjects.

Fascinated with the mysteries of nature, Mrs. Connelly has pursued her interest of what she refers to as "oddball travel" in extraordinary areas of the world—Siberian Eskimo villages, outer islands of French Polynesia, Canada's northwest territories, the Arctic, Baja California Sur, and the Fijis.

"Follow the birds to Victoria" Gulls were
photographed riding a lifeboat stanchion on the
big car-ferry *Queen of Tsawwassen.*

GUIDEBOOK TO VANCOUVER ISLAND

Off the Coast of
Southwest British Columbia

BY DOLLY CONNELLY

WARD RITCHIE PRESS · LOS ANGELES

To the delightful, cussedly independent people of Vancouver Island with the wish that forever may they resist Manifest Destiny, and anything else that comes along. And especially to dear Lyn and John Buckley of the Department of Recreation and Conservation, the A-Watch of the Playtex Princess, and those friendly West Coast ship captains, Esson Young and John Monrufet.

BACK COVER: *Alert Bay, Cormorant Island, an Indian fishing and logging village near the northern tip of Vancouver Island, is famed for its magnificent totems, here photographed in heavy mist, and Kwakiutl Indian artifacts. The location of the small village is beautiful, in the mouth of Queen Charlotte Strait. These totems are in a Kwakiutl Indian graveyard in the heart of the community.*

FRONT COVER: *One of the many attractive beaches at Rebecca Spit Provincial Park on Quadra Island.*

First Printing 1973
COPYRIGHT © 1973 BY DOLLY CONNELLY
Library of Congress Catalog Card Number 72-91494
ISBN 0378-03182-1
Lithographed in the United States of America
by Anderson, Ritchie and Simon, Los Angeles
Maps by Cas Duchow
Color Cover and Black and White Photographs by Author

CONTENTS

CHAPTER   PAGE

Introduction 11
1. *Geology and Geography* 19
2. *The Scant Highways* 21
3. *The Sea-Going Highways* 25
4. *Victoria and Environs* 34
5. *The Shopping Treats* 45
6. *Butchart Gardens* 47
7. *West of Victoria* 50
8. *The Gulfs* 53
9. *The Discovery Islands* 61
10. *Up-Island* 66
11. *Cowichan Indian Country* 67
12. *The Forest Museum* 71
13. *Nanaimo* 74
14. *Forbidden Plateau* 78
15. *Campbell River* 81
16. *On to Kelsey Bay and the Inside Passage* 86
17. *The Playtex Princess* 88
18. *Alert Bay* 92
19. *Lonely Northern Island* 93
20. *The West Coast's Nootka Sound* 99
21. *Cruising on the Uchuck III* 105
22. *Instant Town—Gold River* 110
23. *Strathcona* 113
24. *The West Coast* 117
25. *Port Alberni* 119
26. *The Lady Rose* 121
27. *The Life Saving Trail* 125
28. *Pacific Rim National Park, The Great Beaches and
    That Awesome Road* 129
29. *Ucluelet and Tofino* 136
30. *Where to Stay* 137

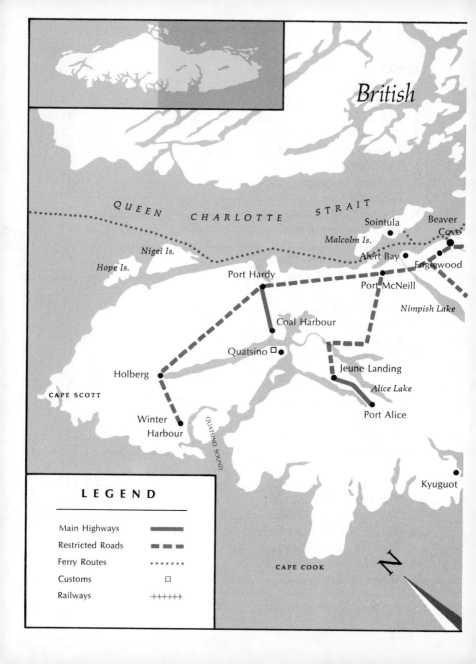

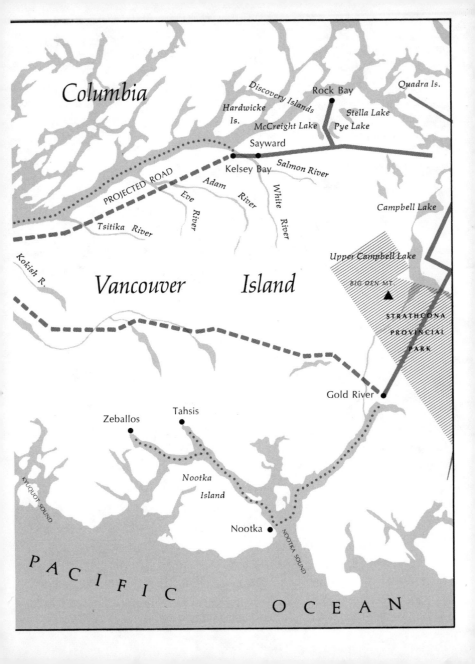

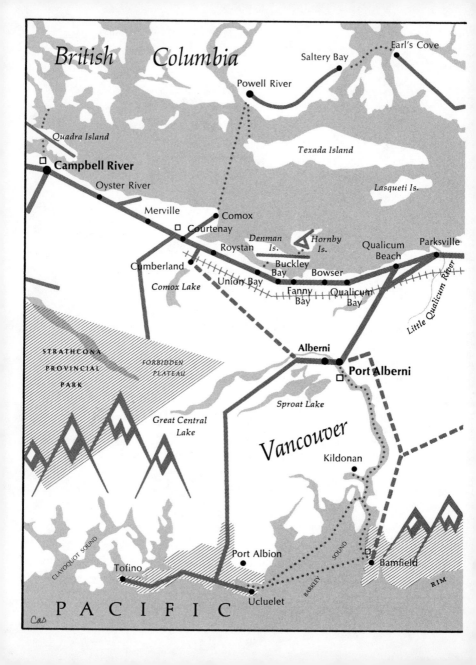

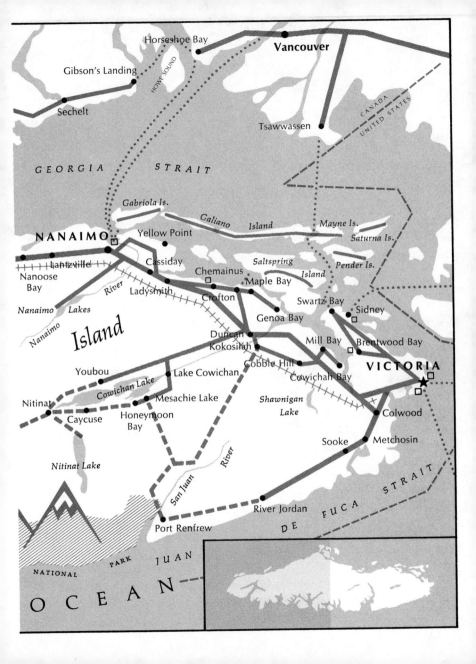

*The waterways of beautiful Rebecca Spit
Provincial Park at Drew Harbor are safe places
for children to play.*

INTRODUCTION

Years ago, the Canadian province of British Columbia began to post a magic legend in the states along the Pacific Coast. The billboards showed nothing but white gulls against a blue sky above the command, "Follow the birds to Victoria".

The genius who thought this one up intended only to increase tourism to the charming city at the toe of Vancouver Island, but he fired such yearning in at least one member of his audience that forever after always I must follow the birds north to Canada.

Once I reached the ultimate point, trudging far out on the ice pack of the Beaufort Sea along Eskimo dog sled tracks so I wouldn't fall through sections deteriorating to brittle candle ice. I climbed up on a pressure ridge and there was absolutely alone with a tremendous bowl of pale nascent sky overhead and nothing at all but that dull, faintly gleaming ice. A couple jaegers were pestering an arctic tern over an open lead, trying to make him drop his fish. I'd followed the birds as far north as we both could go.

I made an important discovery. As you go farther north the littoral becomes lonelier, mystic and alien in stark magnificence; but never is it more beautiful than is the 282 crow-flight mile span of the Pacific coast incorporated in Vancouver Island and its enchanting satellite islands. A love affair begun in childhood rests on solid ground.

I exulted most, I think, in the sound and sight and earthy smell of running water—tides that roared like waterfalls, streams, rivers, lakes, rain, soft grey opalescent light of foggy mornings all were absolute heaven to a child raised in the sere, ochre hills of Southern California. Secondly, there was a kind of intoxication with escape from the mainstream of civilization, a response common to all islands, tangible even to the grammar

11

school set. It is indicative that though I am an avid reader of newspapers, all kinds, once on Vancouver Island I lose interest in a world that has ceased to exist beyond the Prussian blue waters of the Strait of Juan de Fuca, Georgia Strait, Johnstone Strait and the Pacific Ocean. I'm free — that's it — of the troubles of the world, can set down my self-imposed burden of angst in this magic milieu. In Canada I feel very Canadian, a very special feeling.

This rapport with islands began when Father — an easy mark for anybody who smelled of campfires — purchased an island in the Sabine Channel of the Strait of Georgia from a French-Canadian who wandered into his office one day with a lot of fuzzy snapshots of salmon and a persuasive way of incarnating a kind of life for which Father's very soul yearned. Epitome of the grey-flannel-suit and stiff collar clan, Father always saw himself as a kind of natural super-ranger in tune with the wilds, an innate fisherman, hunter, mountaineer, woodsman who would have been right at home at Walden Pond except for the slight handicap of a wife and eight children. Thus the French-Canadian, Pierre, was thought transference in the flesh.

Pierre went through life with a lush, moist-lipped leer for the ladies, his plaid flannel shirt unbuttoned over his curly-haired, convex chest right down to the navel, long eyelashes and a strong mon Dieu accent. He wore round knit caps on the back of his head with shiny black curls fanned up against the red wool all around, and high boots that laced practically to the crotch — altogether a fine figure of a woodsman.

Naturally impulsive Father bought from him his Jervis Island, sight unseen, and hired this alter ego to build upon it a family lodge. Thereafter the entire family was transported en masse by coastal steamer to Victoria, and thence by various means — Esquimalt and Nanaimo Railway, fish boat — to summers in this this family Outward Bound.

12

Butchart Gardens on Tod Inlet of the Saanich Peninsula is world famous, has attracted more than six million visitors to its exotic 25 acres of beauty. The gardens were begun by Mr. and Mrs. Robert Pim Butchart at this spot, a bleak, abandoned limestone quarry, and expanded to four great areas: the English Rose Garden, Italian Garden, Japanese Garden and Sunken Garden. Visitors are welcome year-round.

My mother never got over her fear of the island's "wilderness", expecting at the very least to encounter grizzly bears or wild Indians on its secret trails hidden deep in head-high bracken fern and fir forest. She got in her innings by delaying en route as long as possible in Victoria, laying in the summer's supplies with exasperating, slow deliberation in between visits to English rose gardens, antique shops and cultural events.

I remember most vividly the long, sweet June afternoons trailing Jennie Butchart about her fantastic gardens, marveling at the blue poppy of Tibet and a thousand flower varieties and fragrances we little ones never had known before. In those days visitors were welcomed by the Butcharts as interested friends, and always ended their tour of the gardens with tea at Benvenuto, the Butchart residence, from delicate, near-transparent bone China cups.

Just recently on a hot, bright, over-crowded day in mid-August I returned to Butchart Gardens and once more looked down upon that flamboyant burst of color, the Sunken Gardens in the old limestone quarry that became the center of Jennie Butchart's creative art. Below were busload after busload of visitors on guided tours, waiting their turn to enter the paths. My eyes filled with tears and I turned back, unwilling to alter memory by sharing with the six million people who have walked these paths in recent years. I'll come again in spring and fall, in the quiet seasons when the gardens dream again in comparative solitude.

Other memories stand out clear as a bell. Long walks on the clifftop paths of Beacon Hill Park along Juan de Fuca Strait, the snowy Olympic Range rising in sawtooth ridge against the blue sky, haven't changed. Some of life on Vancouver Island no longer is "different" from North American universality. Yet the Garry oaks still cluster on the hilltop, and in spring the park is a carpet of scatter-planted bulbs in bloom, hundreds of thousands

People come from all over the world for the spectacular Easter blooming of hundreds of thousands of scatter-planted bulbs under the freshly leafing Garry oaks of Beacon Hill Park.

of daffodils and narcissuses contrasted to dogtooth violet and grape hyacinth bending in the wind.

Somewhere in Victoria there still may flourish a Chinese restaurant that seemed to us children the very apogee of glamor. Among its delectable dishes was a sticky dumpling about the size of a softball, filled with pungent bean curd. I saw something like it once in Honolulu's Chinese section, but I've never found it again in many visits to Victoria.

Another changeless is the Empress Hotel. Regrettably the ponderous bathtubs with lion claw feet and "facilities" with overhead tanks long since have been replaced, but there remain the ceremony of afternoon tea in the Edwardian lounge, the conservatory filled with exotic bloom, and the time-honored elegance of dinner in the Empress Room.

Once Mother was forcibly separated from Victoria, which really *was* English in those days, the children's idyll began, a summer as wild and free as children of the gentle Gulf Islands still know today. We had a good thing going for us. Father, infatuated with the salmon fishing, was off daily with Pierre in the one-lunged fishing boat Attaboy. Mother — who did not worry about children's activities that she did not personally observe, doubtless necessary mental therapy for all mothers of eight — retreated to the porch of the lodge to paint pretty pictures of scenery. As long as we turned up regularly for meals and showed no evidence of broken bones, we were on our own, unfettered as the huffy crows, the little wild pigs and bald eagles indigenous to the island.

We discovered thrilling games. At tidal change, all this great inland sea in the northwest corner — Puget Sound and Georgia Strait — moves with the speed of a millrace in certain areas. We had such a phenomenon in Sabine Channel, the narrow body of water between Jervis and neighboring Lasqueti Island. A rowboat caught at the height of the great river of tidal flow zipped along as if pulled by a giant underwater hand. The idea was to ride north on the outrushing tide, thrilled and scared pea-soup green, and then at slack tide hook a ride back into rowing vicinity of Jervis Island with tug and log boom. Texada Island was being logged at that time — still is. Booms departed this big island at fairly frequent intervals heading down the backside of Jervis Island for mainland points.

We little ones tied the painter not to the tug, but to the logs and climbed up on the boom to survey the passing sights, precariously drawing our skinny, brown, bug-bitten legs over the slimy cables. With any luck at all, we soon were spotted by the crews of the tugs who emerged on deck to wave their arms back and forth with shouts of "Get offen there, you little bastids!" Safe at the other end of 200-yard towlines, we lazed on the logs, deaf to shouts and threats, at once defiant of adult authority and cozily en route homeward. For some reason that may have to do with frontier sportsmanship, they never reported us to Father.

We didn't change Jervis, and perhaps that is the ultimate glory of the Vancouver Island archipelago. I flew low over Jervis Island recently and noted no remaining mark of all those long-gone summers. The lichen-covered rocks remain, the madrona and tangles of fern and fir, the sunburned golden meadows, the long narrow points of eroded sandstone extend-ing outward in pocketed seaworn shelves to protect coves of pure enchantment, the concentric swirls from emerald to the ink blue of great depth surrounding the little chains of tree-tufted islands extending from either end of Jervis. The build-ings long since have been engulfed by returning forest. Seas have swept away the dock. We might never have been. Nature is a tough old babe in these parts. Thus isolated lands are not really much altered since a poetic Spanish mapmaker and explorer named Francisco Eliza in 1790 ventured through the

Strait of Juan de Fuca and reported "an unknown labyrinth of verdant isles" sky-floating above beds of pearly mist.

If this book has purpose, it is the sharing of people and places and pleasures that I have loved through a lifetime of exploring Vancouver Island. Some of it is highly personal detailing of experiences nobody much knows about but the locals. Year after year more of this special, vernal world becomes accessible as logging roads come off the restricted list, highways are extended and new ferries put into service. Yet those fjord-slashed fastnesses, the soaring mountains, the lonely brave settlements pushing back the wilderness with little more than an axe, a fish pole and a prayer, never will be tamed in entirety, never wholly joined to the staid, everyday world. I find great comfort in this, in the splendor of all the up-island frontier lands.

It is a sincere wish that this guide book will erase some of the widely-held conviction that "Victoria is Vancouver Island — if you've been there you've seen it all". Victoria is the gateway, the opening fanfare to a fresh, new island world waiting for discovery.

I GEOLOGY AND GEOGRAPHY

This glacier scoured land features a mild climate unique to Canada.

Vancouver Island once was part of the sea bottom, elevated by a long series of volcanic eruptions. The island's stunning form, the great range of 7000-foot mountains rising through its center, the deep fjords of the west coast which come near to cutting the island into six parts, the gently sloping eastern shore which abruptly turns mountainous in a series of ranges north of Discovery Passage, were created by moving ice.

In the last great Ice Age, glaciers thought to have been 6000 feet in depth scoured the young mountains, leaving in their wake terrain of infinite variety. Narrow inlets more than a thousand feet in depth, long sweet valleys of lush growth, innumerable sparkling lakes, alpine peaks such as 7219-foot Golden Hinde, 7200-foot Elkhorn, 7095-foot Victoria Peak, Mount Albert Edward at 6868 feet, Forbidden Plateau, the wild tyrannosaur-toothed Franklin Range of the northern part of the island and many more, all bear testimony to the might of flowing ice.

The island's climate is mild, influenced by the Pacific Ocean, unique to Canada and reason enough for the emergence of Vancouver Island as a kind of Valhalla to retired prairie wheat farmers. Average rainfall in Victoria, well into the "banana belt" protected by the rain-squeezing heights of the Olympics, is only about twenty-seven inches. The Greater Victoria area has 282 frost-free days, the longest growing season in Canada. The wet west coast, out there on the open Pacific, hits a high at Zeballos with an annual rainfall around 250 inches. Coastal islands show the same variation. The snug Gulf Islands off the east coast and north in Johnstone and Queen Charlotte Straits enjoy the weather-protection of mountains against the westerlies. The wilderness islands of the west coast, most of them clustered at the mouths of immense inlets facing the open sea, remain largely uninhabited tangles of salal and great trees.

The air is the only vantage point from which to gain comprehension of the fantastic number of America's San Juan Islands and Canada's adjoining Gulfs, which continue the broad syncline well up the east coast of Vancouver Island. Their setting, in vast amphitheatre of great mountains tacked down by the volcanic peaks of the North Cascades and Canada's continuation of the cordillera in its Coast Range, is breath-taking from a plane. So exalting is flight over the islands that a sensitive Victoria doctor for years has prescribed flight as a specific for malaise of the spirit.

"No one can fly over this fantasy without comprehending that God's still in His world," he explained to me.

It is believed that Vancouver Island once joined the mainland, separating in some submarine convulsion in the Paleozoic era, a dark age of dinosaurs, of marine and flying reptiles and ganoid fishes. The satellite island chain then emerged from the sedimentary ooze, its peaks inundated by glaciers and again submerged by the weight of ice back into their sea trough.

Still above water are the tops of these drowned mountains, islands with enchanting Spanish names like Saturna, Galiano, Valdes, Gabriola, Quadra and Cortes, their highest points deeply striated and polished by glacial movement. The archipelago still is shrugging off remembered pressure of that incalculable burden of ice, still lifting an occasional uncharted reef out of the depths. The slow uplift is apparent in remarkably uniform wave-cut benches of honeycomb sandstone at elevations of twenty to forty feet above high tide line ringing many a rugged coast.

20

2   THE SCANT HIGHWAYS

Road construction is virtually impossible in some areas.

Even a quick glance at a map of Vancouver Island will reveal a startling fact. This largest island lying off the coast of western North America, 282 miles in length, an average of sixty miles in width, a land mass of about 12,500 square miles (inclusive of islands the total area is 13,250 square miles) has remarkably few highways. Road construction on the west coast except for short spans around the southern tip to Port Renfrew, twenty-six miles along the marvelous beaches of the Esowista Peninsula from Ucluelet to Tofino, and brief restricted (logging) roads to Quatsino Sound communities at the northern tip, is an engineer's nightmare. Probably it never will be possible to drive clear around Vancouver Island.

On the east coast, splendid paved highway extends north 215 miles from Victoria (Trans-Canada No. 1 to Nanaimo, after that Provincial Highway No. 19, generally referred to simply as Island Highway) to Kelsey Bay — way up there on Johnstone Strait. Within the next four years, this highway will be extended inland — to circumvent a series of mountain ranges dropping abruptly into the strait — to Beaver Cove, there joining present paved highway to Port Hardy.

Two major paved highways cross the island, one from Parksville twenty-nine miles to Port Alberni at the head of Alberni Inlet, an arm of Barkley Sound. It's a great route, pungent with the earthy smell of dense ferns, moss and wet rocks, conifers and salal. En route is one of the loveliest of Vancouver Island's many parks, Cathedral Grove of MacMillan Park, a towering virgin forest saved for posterity when the area was logged. The second cross-island highway meanders from Campbell River fifty-seven miles to the "instant town" Gold River, and thence another eight miles (paved) to the headwaters of Muchalat Inlet of Nootka Sound.

From Port Alberni a fairly notorious road, Provincial Highway No. 4, extends to the Long Beach span and from Ucluelet to Tofino — the area now under development as the Pacific Rim National Park, first of Canada's great national parks on the Pacific Coast. Sixty-seven miles in length, a one-time logging road, it now is paved except for a tooth and tire-shattering, narrow, winding seventeen-mile span above Sproat Lake. Taken with due care and at snail's pace, it presents no real difficulties. Within a year at most, this one span of the Port Alberni — Long Beach highway will be completed, probably engineered down off the summit of the Klitsa Mountains. For all the chuckholes, the view is marvelous.

The Campbell River-Gold River road, Provincial Highway No. 28, offers a bonus — a paved thirty-mile drive down the exquisite beauty of Buttle Lake in Strathcona Provincial Park reaching two splendid camping areas and affording views of the highest peaks of Vancouver Island.

On the south along the Strait of Juan de Fuca paved road (Provincial Highway No. 14) extends from Victoria to River Jordan. The final span to Port Renfrew is graded gravel, eminently worth traveling in a period of summer's minus tides for the wonder known as Botany Bay.

The restricted logging road from Port Renfrew on the southwest coast of the island through to Shawnigan Lake and junction with Trans-Canada No. 1, some day will be opened permanently to the public, as will be the restricted road from Youbou on Cowichan Lake to the west coast at Bamfield. Other restricted roads, barred to public use until logging trucks have come to roost after five-thirty or six o'clock in the late afternoon except

22

on weekends and holidays, can be recommended only to the intrepid adventurer with four-wheel-drive vehicle, a passion to fish lakes that never before have known the flick of fly fishing rod, camping gear, strong taste for dust and iron nerves.

This includes the restricted road from Port Alberni to Bamfield, that from Gold River north to Beaver Cove, the one from Port Hardy to Winter Harbour and others on the northern tip to Port Alice. Most especially do not attempt the horror from Gold River to Tahsis in an automobile designed for satin-smooth freeways. Even the locals admit, "The mountain shows through on this one."

Canadians, who will drive over absolutely anything without a qualm, having been indoctrinated in "pioneer roads", dismiss hazards with a laugh. "Oh you'll taste a little dust," they'll say, forgetting to mention that the bald-headed eagles think twice before attempting flight over the area. Best source of information on the condition of dubious roads, restricted roads, and roads under construction is the drivers of omnipresent Vancouver Island Coach Lines who go everywhere and, bless their hearts, often have taken me places I was fearful of driving on my own. If Vancouver Island Coach Lines can't get there, a good rule of thumb to follow is go by plane, boat, bicycle, horse or on foot.

Don't fear the short spans inland from Duncan on the east coast to Lake Cowichan. They're paved, opening up a lovely area of freshwater swimming, sailing, and trout fishing. Roads of the east coast islands are graded gravel. They offer no problems other than the need to watch for deer and bicycling vacationers in the early morning and evening hours.

There are no roads on west coast islands, where Indian names are as rich and beautiful on the tongue as the Spanish on the east coast — Clo-oose, Nitinat, Ecoole, Wickaninnish, Maquinna, Clayoquot, Muchalat, Tlupana, Ahousat, Quatsino. Esquimalt & Nanaimo Railway still runs a little diesel-powered

23

passenger Dayliner daily except Sundays. They're on the old route between Victoria and Courtenay with plenty of way points, fun for children who've never ridden a train before.

There are thousands of beauty spots in the Gulf Islands, this one a boat-launching site on South Pender Island looking across the narrow channel to North Pender Island.

3 THE SEA-GOING HIGHWAYS

Vancouver Island's ferry system is among the best in the world.

Even more important than the highway system, now rapidly enlarging, are the British Columbia and Department of Highways Ferries, a perfectly glorious fleet ranging all the way from the elegant and beautiful Queen of Prince Rupert to such little charmers of the inland seas as the MV Sointula Queen and the MV Texada Queen. As the ferry system regularly is enlarged with new craft and routes, one of the first aids to request of the Department of Travel Industry, address 1019 Wharf Street, Victoria, is a current B.C. Ferries schedule.

Other absolute necessities for visitors are Vancouver Island Coach Lines schedules, the British Columbia Tourist Directory (which will tell you everything you always wanted to know but were afraid to ask, from accommodation information including rates, to a list of guide-outfitters for big game hunting); a new map of Vancouver Island showing the highway surfaces, the beautiful map and descriptions of Provincial Parks and the current Calendar of Events.

The ferry schedule will blow your mind. *Nowhere on earth* is public transportation via automobile ferries more extensive, better run, more concerned with trying to get aboard every last car on the dock even at the height of tourist season, July and August. I love them, every one, from the dear pokey Island Princess to the Queen of Esquimalt, from Gabriola Island's Westwood to Thetis Island's Ethel Hunter. Other loves for their skills and courtesy are Pacific Western Airlines, which flies on regular schedule as far up-island as Port Hardy and on frequent schedule (four flights daily) between Vancouver, Victoria and

25

Seattle; Victoria Flying Service which serves a whole string of island points; Canada's Airwest Airlines (not Hughes), which flies to fairly inaccessible interior island points like Vernon Lake; Alert Bay Air Services, which reaches settlements of northern Vancouver Island and the mainland coast; and numerous small charter services — always superbly staffed — which will take you most anywhere.

Let's detail the ferries, because you can't get your car to the island any other way despite long-ago plans to bridge Seymour Narrows and build a series of causeways connecting a slew of islands to the mainland. It is important to think of them as extensions of the highways with a deal of glamorous sightseeing thrown in, good also for walk-on day trips. There are eight points of mainland departure: Washington state's Port Angeles, Anacortes and Seattle, British Columbia's Tsawwassen (pronounced Sah-wah-sen), Horseshoe Bay at West Vancouver and downtown Vancouver, Powell River and Prince Rupert.

Ferries departing Port Angeles head directly across the Strait of Juan de Fuca for Victoria's Inner Harbour, setting passengers off almost in the lap of the Parliament Buildings, Provincial Museum and Empress Hotel, handsome heart of the city. Short-term visitors don't even need their cars, for Victoria's downtown area is eminently strollable and great attractions such as Butchart Gardens can be reached easily by near-continuous coach schedules. Besides there are Victoria's bright red double-decker London buses and horse-drawn tally-hos, just begging to be ridden to all the nearby attractions.

The Port Angeles-Inner Harbour run is via Black Ball Transport's MV Coho, which makes two trips daily in winter, at least four in summer. Canadian Pacific's Princess Marguerite from early May to the last of September travels daily between Seattle and Inner Harbour. From mid-June to early September, the Princess Marguerite adds Port Angeles to her daily ports-of-

26

call, sailing first from Seattle to Victoria, then to Port Angeles, will hold car space for persons with reservations — vital in July and August, over Memorial Day and Labor Day weekends. Ask about the Princess Marguerite's overnight excursions at reduced rates.

Washington State Ferries runs two trips daily from Anacortes, at the northern tip of Fidalgo Island, through the beauteous San Juan Archipelago to Sidney at the tip of the Saanich Peninsula, an easy nineteen-mile drive over the freeway to Victoria. At the height of summer travel, the weekend overflow of vehicles waiting to board ferries at Port Angeles and Anacortes can be enough to throw a vacation into a tailspin, but there's always walk-on space and buses waiting to take you to Victoria. The Washington ferries do not provide adequate service for the thousands of Northwest visitors in the summer months. If you must go through the San Juans on a summer weekend, be prepared to wait your turn — not hours, but even a full day. I've never understood why the British Columbia ferry system, an efficient money maker, always remains in the black, while Washington's service costs the taxpayers a bundle. And serves a poor cup of coffee.

The British Columbia Ferry Authority in 1960 began fast hourly service seven in the morning to ten in the evening from Tsawwassen in the southern extremity of the Fraser River Delta through Active Pass — considered by many of the appreciative the single most exhilarating passage in all the islands — to Swartz Bay, near Sidney. The big ferries each can take 140 cars and 960 passengers at a time on the one hour and forty minute run. They have acquired a considerable reputation for good food in their dining salons and cafeterias, cleanliness and service. Canadians do these things beautifully. The facilities on this route are augmented by a coach service on alternate hours all day and every day from the bus terminal at Vancouver to the bus terminal at Victoria. In fact coaches run all the big ferry routes.

Four B. C. Ferries connect the West Vancouver port at Horseshoe Bay with Departure Bay, just north of Nanaimo, sailing as frequently as at thirty-minute intervals during the height of the day's demand. Again, coach and ferry combine for downtown to downtown service with connections to all island and mainland points. Canadian Pacific's Princess ships on varying summer and winter schedule sail three round-trip crossings daily from downtown Vancouver (Pier A-3) to Nanaimo on Vancouver Island.

Powell River, well up the Sunshine Coast just about as far north as you can drive along the inland sea from Vancouver, is connected via the MV Comox Queen to Little River on Vancouver Island, near Comox. Operated by the Department of Highways, the Powell River-Comox summer schedule calls for seven crossings.

Lastly among mainland to island ferries — and by no means least — is the magnificent Queen of Prince Rupert, reigning monarch of the entire fleet, which sails summers and winters on varying schedules from Prince Rupert, northernmost large seaport of British Columbia at the terminus of Route Sixteen, to Kelsey Bay on Vancouver Island at the present terminus of the paved Island Highway. This new service, which began in the summer of 1966, carries ninety cars and 430 passengers some 330 miles (one way) through the famed Inside Passage, a glorious twenty-hour sea journey comparable to passage up the west coast of Norway. Connections are made with the Alaska Ferries at Prince Rupert. At the height of the summer season, reservations are absolutely necessary, even for walk-ons. Write British Columbia Ferries, Box 1388, 816 Wharf Street, Victoria, for reservations, schedules and fares.

British Columbia Ferries' rates for the short trips from main-

*A delightful island-hopping day may be spent in the Gulf Islands
on the car-ferry Mayne Queen, which visits Saturna, Mayne,
Galiano and North Pender Island, picking up and discharging
numbers of backpackers and bicycling vacationists.
Bicycles, always popular in Victoria, are the ideal vehicle for
traveling the few roads of the Gulf Islands, each of which
has a provincial park and campsite as well as small resorts.
Here the Mayne Queen pulls in to Montague Harbor of
Galiano Island, one of the loveliest of them all.*

*Long before the sun has risen, Long Harbour on
Salt Spring Island is a place of mystery and
enthralling beauty. One of the big Tsawwassen
car-ferries overnights at Long Harbour, picking up
passengers in the early morning for calls at
Pender, Mayne and Galiano Islands en route to
the British Columbia mainland.*

land to island have not changed in years and may be set down as (one way) five dollars for car, two dollars for each passenger, one dollar for children five to eleven years of age, babies free, and fares from three dollars and thirty-cents for an eight-foot trailer to sixty-five cents per foot for oversize trailers. This includes Tsawwassen to Swartz Bay, Horseshoe Bay to Departure Bay.

The best way to comprehend the wealth of sea-going possibilities is a study of schedules, summer and winter. (Service is slightly curtailed in the off-season.) Otherwise you may miss island-hopping combinations via the Gulf Islands Services. Currently routes are from Tsawwassen to Long Harbour on Salt Spring Island with ports of call at Otter Bay on North Pender Island, Saturna at Saturna Island, Village Bay on Mayne Island, and Sturdies Bay on Galiano Island; from Swartz Bay on Vancouver Island to Fulford Harbour on Salt Spring Island; and from Crofton, near Duncan on Vancouver Island, to Vesuvius Bay on Salt Spring Island. With a little logistics planning and a few changes from ferry to ferry, you can see a great deal of this special world in a day. Washington's Mount Baker, northernmost of the Cascade Range volcanic cones, dominates the mountain complex viewed from the islands.

The major routes are augmented by Department of Highways Ferries which tootle from east coast points of Vancouver Island in the delightful Coastal Ferry Service. Thus the MV Westwood sails continuously between Nanaimo and Gabriola Island; the MV Catherine Graham between Buckley Bay and Denman Island with continuation to Hornby Island; the MV Ethel Hunter from Chemainus to Thetis Island with request port of call at Kuper Island; the MV Quadra Queen II from Campbell river to Quathiaski Cove on Quadra Island; the MV Cortes Queen from Heriot Bay on Quadra Island to Whaletown on Cortes Island; the MV Texada Queen from Westview, just south

31

of Powell River on the mainland coast, to Blubber Bay on Texada Island; the MV Sointula Queen from Sointula on Malcolm Island in Queen Charlotte Strait to Alert Bay on Cormorant Island and Port McNeill on Vancouver Island; and MV Lasqueti Queen from Parksville to Lasqueti Island.

Hold on! We have by no means exhausted all the possibilities for thrilling sea trips on Vancouver Island. There's a busy little car ferry that pops back and forth across beautiful Saanich Inlet from Brentwood Bay near the Butchart Gardens to Mill Bay on the north side, connecting easily to Trans-Canada Highway No. 1. My all-time favorite, MV Island Princess, sails every afternoon from Kelsey Bay up Johnstone Strait to the northern communities of Beaver Cove, Alert Bay and Sointula. Called "the Playtex Princess" by her aficionados, this car-ferry now is a catamaran, victim of a million-dollar three-way stretch in all directions to accommodate the increasing use of this route.

Though her crews stow cars aboard with such jigsaw puzzle dexterity that only rarely must they leave would-be travelers back on the dock, reservations for the Island Princess ardently are recommended. It's a long drive to Kelsey Bay, and bitter disappointment for those who can't get aboard the Island Princess on day of choice. This particular ferry has no special busy season as she is prime means of transport down to the bright lights for all the loggers, miners, and fishermen of the rugged north end of the island year-around.

No discussion of motorship service is complete without mention of Alberni Marine Transportation Company, which operates the MV Lady Rose out of Port Alberni for Ucluelet on the west coast with ports of call at Kildonan, Sarita and Nahmint, and from Port Alberni to Bamfield at the southern extremity of Barkley Sound. Schedules may be obtained by writing the company at P.O. Box 188, Port Alberni.

A similar freight-passenger-mail service, Nootka Sound

Service Limited, sailing out of the head of Muchalat Inlet near Gold River into the far reaches of the arms of Nootka Sound with ports of call at Zeballos, Tahsis, Esperanza, Little Zeballos, Ceepeecee, Green Logging, Sand Point, Kendrick Arm, Plumper Harbour, Mooyah Bay and Blowhole Bay, is a memorable two-day experience in wilderness exploration. In the summer months, Nootka Sound's MV Uchuck III turns on a twice-weekly one-day cruise to Friendly Cove at the mouth of Nootka Sound to the spot where the modern history of British Columbia began on March 29, 1778, with the landing of Captain James Cook. For schedules, the address is Nootka Sound Service, P.O. Box 28, Port Alberni.

Both of these incomparable journeys — that of the Lady Rose and the Uchuck III — will be detailed later in the section *The West Coast*.

4 VICTORIA AND ENVIRONS

The southern tip of the island.

For some reason that leaves me slack-jawed with amazement, the great bulk of American visitors consider that Victoria, capital of British Columbia, is Vancouver Island—all of it. They also cling to a belief that this exquisitely located city, now burgeoning with a wall of high-rise apartments and hotels in old James Bay, looking out upon the Strait of Juan de Fuca, is still a "little bit of Olde England". Now I'll admit that Victoria runs about seventy percent British, with rumbling Scots burrs music to the ear almost everywhere. But as the population of Greater Victoria surges above 200,000 it no longer is anybody's "little bit". Sad that it had to grow, with inevitable alteration of its charm.

But it has character all its own: a smattering of western frontier, a heaven of interests to explore, tremendous physical beauty, a large percentage of wealthy elderly, limpit-like attachment to fake Tudor architecture and thatched roofs, a stuffy British colonial society still based here and there on "good family name", i.e. good British name; strong emphasis upon the splendidly original art of west coast Indians, a lively history still very much in evidence, an incredible number of parks and flower gardens, outdoor sports of the fishing, yachting, field hockey, golfing, folk dancing, gymkhana and horse show, dog show, classic car rally, curling and turkey shoot varieties; lifted-pinkie culture, the best antique shopping west of Quebec, an interesting waterfront, and proliferating claptrap pseudo-Disneylands on the outskirts that a firm city government should

34

have kept in check. All this, and sunshine too. No wonder that honeymooners of a huge area think-Victoria.

We live on the Olympic Peninsula just across the Strait. For decades it has been our custom to visit Victoria over Easter for the burst of bulb bloom on Beacon Hill and in the commercial fields of the Saanich Peninsula from which more than a million dozen daffodils are flown in spring to eastern Canada. Again we come in fall for peace and quiet, now that Victoria has been returned to the Victorians, vine maple is reddening on hillsides softened by morning mist, and spawning salmon are making their way up bright rivers.

This summer we did a strange thing: sailed over in mid-August on the most frantic day on the Port Angeles ferries in eleven years, quite deliberately without reservations, to test Victorian tourist facilities at height of season. Happily, the city has enough diversions to disperse its visitors. There were only a few joggers and strollers, as example, on the clifftop paths of Beacon Hill.

There are cautions. If you must come in July or August, trot immediately to the Tourist Bureau on Government Street, across from the Empress Hotel, check everything you want to do and make all possible advance reservations. That done, drive out the Gorge Road (Motel Row, Island Highway 1-A) and settle in at the first reasonably attractive motel with a vacancy sign. If you put it off until evening, I have news for you. Did you bring sleeping bags? The nearest provincial park is Goldstream, and all 153 camping units are likely to be filled.

In the quiet seasons, we prefer Oak Bay's Beach Hotel. In downtown Victoria it's the Executive House, Surf Motor Hotel, Wilson Motor Inn or the convenient Belleville Street inns facing Inner Harbour, near the Parliament Buildings and within easy walking distance of the Canadian Pacific docks. At Esquimalt, across Victoria Harbour, a charmer in Anne Hathaway country is the Olde England Inn where Shakespeare and family could move right in without shock to either playwright or hotel staff. The dining room at Olde England is strong for trifles, roast beef and Yorkshire pudding, and toasted crumpets.

Speaking of season on Vancouver Island, the crowds turn off like magic after Labor Day and won't be back en masse until mid-June. Canadian schools close in late June, far later than those of the United States. Most accommodations switch to winter rates. Keep alert to highly appealing special opportunities that turn up regularly in the fall. For instance the elegant Empress Hotel turns on its mini-holidays, three days with breakfasts and dinners and a tour of the city thrown in. Rate is just sixty-three dollars for two, about half the summer tariff. Victoria in season can be expensive.

The 136-foot MV Marabell runs fall cruises through the Gulf Islands in September and October at reasonable rate: one hundred ten dollars for a five-day cruise, eighty-eight dollars for four days. Meals are luxurious, the sun deck space ample, the cabins comfortable for a maximum of twenty-two guests. There are no extras. It's next best to cruising your own yacht. Write Lacerte Holdings Limited, 631 Langford Street, Victoria, for brochure and reservations, which should be made well in advance.

The idea is beauty, and exploration of uninhabited islands. The remainder of a season starting May first, the Marabell follows the great salmon fishing waters south from the Prince Rupert area, exploring the inlets as its passengers fish in a fleet of powered small boats with the advantage of a kind of mobile paradise.

Incidentally, the rate of exchange of American funds is in daily state of flux. You'll get a fair break from chain gasoline stations and large supermarkets, rarely from hotels. Exchange at banks, which you'll find everywhere—even at Alert Bay. And don't think you're being robbed when you pull into gas stations.

In Canada it's the imperial gallon, about one-fifth more generous than the American gallon.

There's also the question of weekday Canadian closures. Monday and Wednesday whole and half-day store closures still are widely observed. Plan shopping with this in mind, and with due regard for Canadian national holidays. Most holidays are the same as those in the United States. Those that throw Americans are Victoria Day, anniversary of the official birthday of Queen Victoria on the Monday closest to May 24th; Dominion Day, always July 1st; and Thanksgiving celebrated on the second Monday in October. Chinese markets *never* close, doing a land office business when the big stores are shut down, at considerably higher prices.

Canadian whiskey is excellent, the beer outstanding, but avoid local wines in the government liquor stores. They're so bad that Canada has few winos, running to beer drunks. Australian wines, which can be ordered in hotels and restaurants, are on a par with good California labels, both red and white.

Well over one-fifth of Victoria's citizens are over-sixty-fives. The farther north you go on the island, the more rigorous grows its way of life, the younger its people. There's an odd thing about Victoria girls. There appear to be few middlewomen. Goodie Twoshoes types, obviously the product of a fairly circumscribed country-estate British culture, are very much in evidence at horse and dog events. In contrast, in the city's restored nineteenth century courts, a conspicuous swath of the female young are dirty of bare foot, aggressively hip, way out. Up-island, outdoor-loving, sports-minded girls predominate.

Definition of the ideal holiday varies as much as human personality. One day I stopped at a Victoria travel agency and requested ideas for "the perfect weekend on Vancouver Island". Soon everyone handy, including the customers, was promoting his own version. Discussion foundered when a handsome young

37

man, leering in the direction of a C-cup receptionist, plumped for locking couples up in hotel rooms.

"Oh, you can't write about *that!*" protested the travel agent, looking a bit faint while C-cup blushed prettily. But the young man is right in a way. It isn't so much where you are as whom you're with. I'm ignorant of Canadian prowess in the field of romance, but this I do know: they're great company, often warmly witty and remarkably well informed. And they like Americans, generally speaking.

It's an older generation's monumental aloofness to change that safeguards the dominant Scots-English heritage, that and the buffer of surrounding seas. Regularly every afternoon there descends from a small flotilla of antique town cars at the carriage entrance of the Empress a score or more of dowagers, crusty with diamonds and dignity. They take their habitual tables in the lobby and under the lush fuchsia baskets in the solarium and there dot Sevilla marmalade on crumpets and sip their tea, completely unruffled by the presence of tourists, jeans-clad teenagers hitch-hiking across Canada, bearded barefoot hippies and other impedimenta common to Victoria in summer. They do their thing too, and it's wonderful to see.

I fell in step with a wiry old gentleman, clad in tartan tam and tasseled knickers, marching a park trail. He was shaken right down to his spatted boots by my admission that I'd never seen Queen Victoria's black beehive bonnet, resting snugly in the Parliament Archives in close company with the Polynesian dagger that murdered Captain Cook in the "Sandwich Isles" in 1779.

"Bless my soul!" he fretted. "Extraordinary! Why, you've missed the best of it!"

Later I lolled on the roof of Sealand of the Pacific at Oak Bay, Canada's largest and most elaborate oceanarium and marine show. An obliging staff member had boosted us up to take photographs out over Oak Bay Marina, an impressive gathering of pleasure, charter, and party fishing boats. Down below an engaging white killer whale named Chimo went through her paces with the aplomb of Olympian Mark Spitz. Seals and sea lions, carried away by this thespian grace, set up a cacophony of barking strong enough to topple us off the roof.

Suddenly I was struck by the incongruity of it all — a bustling tourist mecca right inside Oak Bay's "Tweed Curtain" in full sight of ivy-covered Tudor mansions and rose-bordered walks where ancient basset hounds are paraded by equally ancient masters; Oak Bay of the Victoria Golf Club, one of the most beautiful links in Canada, cricket teams, and the Royal Victoria Yacht Club of Swiftsure Race renown.

"Don't they complain about Sealand — the traffic and noise?" I asked.

"You mean the Green Stamp crowd? You bet they do. They call the cops all night to stop the seals from barking. You ever try to tell a seal to quit barking?"

And then there's the late lamented Queenie, a languid-gaited, somnolent work horse who for many years pulled a cart for the gathering of fallen leaves on Beacon Hill. Queenie now rests under an elegant headstone in the animal shelter, visited faithfully by Victorians who remember her fondly. One Easter we were in Victoria coincident with the retirement of Queenie. She had been replaced by a machine in which park employees had no faith.

"It's no dommed good," they confided darkly while indignant gentlemen, clusters of school children, and outraged dowagers protested in the Letters column of the Victoria Times. A rumour had got around that Queenie was destined for the glue factory. The desperate Parks Department, which intended only to retire this somewhat pixilated and overfat member to the deer shelter, flinched before sacks of mail containing copies of "The

Horse's Prayer". It did no good to protest that Queenie had it made.

Various Victorians did their duty, checking her whereabouts daily. Children fed her pizzas, popsickles and potato chips with such abandon that soon Queenie was shockingly obese. Like a corpulent matron, once down, she had to be helped to her feet. In the interests of equine dietary discretion, Queenie was moved back from the fence, out of reach of loving little hands for a Weight Watchers interlude. She died, eventually, of plain senility.

In contrast to this facet of the Victorian character, the city once called "the only cemetery with street lights" has begun to swing. Restoration of nineteenth century courts in the downtown area has much to do with it, because no sooner were Bastion Square, Trounce Alley, and Nootka Court (more sedate are the new Heritage Court and Centennial Square) restored and their shops filled with far out merchandise than the whole areas became once again vital, vibrant, filled with life and laughter, miniatures of Vancouver's restored Gastown.

Art-minded members of the hippie colony took up sidewalk residence, displaying surprisingly fine craftsmanship with leather, jewelry, macrame, bead work and cartoon sketches. The old Law Chambers and Village Square are haven to some of the best craftsmen in western Canada.

There's always a folk music group singing in Bastion Square, and a chess game underway. The Coach and Four steak house is located in an historic warehouse of Bastion Square, one of the city's oldest buildings which once serviced sailing vessels tied up at the foot of the square. Le Coq au Vin is a pleasant place to lunch here.

Barbary Banjo in the Square entertains with a Roaring Twenties blast, but puts emphasis upon food. Nootka Square houses Felice's Ristorante, a posh Italian restaurant serving all the favorites from lasagna to zabaglione, with dancing and entertainment nightly. The Wig & Dickie in the Wilson Inn (long known for its Old Bailey dining room) is the reincarnation of a Scottish country pub, loud and funny, with Scots piper, good food, sing-alongs, dancing, and entertainment.

Other goodies are the Gay Nineties, a spare rib house in the Cherry Bank Hotel; Chez Ernest, Swiss Chalet on the route to the Swartz Bay ferries (Highway No. 17); The Cossack on Fort Street (far eastern specialties); The Captain's Palace on Belleville Street, overlooking Inner Harbour; The Nutshell on Fort Street, quiet and sedate; The Beachcomber Polynesian restaurant off Douglas on Broughton Street; and McPherson's Steak House in Centennial Square. There's still a Chinese Village Restaurant out Douglas Street near the Mayfair Shopping Center. The landlocked S.S. Princess Mary on Harbour Road can be good fun.

I doubt that Victoria ever will acquire fame as a true gourmet's paradise, but these are a decided improvement over the dreary cuisine that once prevailed. I asked husband and son to recall the finest meal they'd ever had on Vancouver Island.

"The crumbly, aged Cheddar at the Cheese & Wein Shop."

"English licorice and banbury tarts from the little shops on the east side of Government Street."

"Barkley Sound shrimp that we bought at the Argyle Street dock in Port Alberni."

"The strawberries big as plums from a roadside stand on Saanich Peninsula, so fragrant we ate them right out of the boxes sand and all."

"Barbecued lamb on Saturna Island."

"No, I mean *meals*—not just treats!"

Son Joel mulled. "Remember when friend Howard and I went camping in the provincial parks all over the island, and asked you for some simple stuff with clams and oysters and geoducks to fix over campfires? Well, those are the best meals I've ever had on Vancouver Island."

The dishes he holds in such fond memory are an easy clam chowder made by adding the chopped meat of geoducks (giant clams native to the Northwest) to a couple cans of vegetable soup, eggs scrambled with lots of butter clams, chopped clams stirred into instant mashed potatoes thinned to bisque consistency with clam nectar and milk, and fritters made by stirring up pancake mix with lots of eggs and adding at least an equal amount of clams. The oyster recipe calls for roasting them on a grill over hardwood coals until they open, then dousing the delectable sizzling meat with butter and lemon juice. Victoria's cuisine may have some way to go, or perhaps there's no way of equalling the enjoyment of a meal prepared out of doors from fresh, wild foods you've gathered with joy in the hunt.

For all the new aspects of Victoria, the old pleasures remain. Not to be missed are Antique Row along Fort Street, the Maritime Museum in the Law Courts Building, Bastion Square; Parliament Buildings, the Archives and gardens; Inner Harbour, over 600 lamp pole flower baskets which actually receive fan mail, the summit view from Malahat Drive, Craigdarroch Castle, the great house with tones of Balmorality built in the 1880s by Robert Dunsmuir (who made a fortune in coal mining on the island) and now the home of the School of Music; Government House—the gardens are open to the public—residence of the lieutenant-governor, representative of the Queen, home to visiting royalty; the totems of Thunderbird Park, harbour tours in wheezing launches, shops of European flair, gardens ablaze with the artistry of mad hedge clippers and rosarians transplanted out of the English countryside to a benign climate where the season of bloom never ends, the Undersea Gardens in the Inner Harbour, the Royal London Wax Museum, the Classic Car Museum just behind the Empress Hotel, and best of all, the Provincial Museum, Canada's finest showplace of Indian art and dioramas of wildlife.

Indian influence is very strong on Vancouver Island, which once was occupied (and still is) by Indians of the southern Kwakiutl, Haida, Nootka, Coast Salish and Cowichan tribes with numerous subdivisions into tribal boundaries and village settlements. Almost every town along Island Highway displays Indian art, the finest north of Victoria: a longhouse and totems on Campbell River's waterfront. Excellent Indian art fashioned by modern craftsmen after the old ways is available to the collector in shops of Victoria, Koksilah, Nanaimo, and Campbell River. Totem poles, ranging in height from a few inches to six or more feet, carved of unpainted wood and of argillite, sometimes set with abalone shell; figures of animals, birds and fishes, models of potlatch dishes, masks and carved canoe paddles are bold and vigorous examples of a renewed appreciation of Northwest Indian art.

*A Cowichan Indian sweater knitter, one of the
finest, enjoys the companionship of a small
grandson as she works. No two sweaters ever are
alike, but follow the artistic ideas of their creators.
Patterns are worked in natural white and black
wool and shades of grey made by mixing the two.
No true Indian sweater ever is dyed, as the
process would remove natural water-shedding
lanolin from the wool.*

5 THE SHOPPING TREATS

A shopping haven for connoisseurs of treasure.

The shops of Victoria are not for bargain hunters, but for connoisseurs of treasure. They offer old glass, silver, bone China, Wedgewood, Spode, Toby jugs, out-of-print books, old maps and charts; wonderful knitting yarns (The Beehive Wool on Fort Street), antique jewelry, exotic blended teas and spices, and incredibly good pound cakes and toffees in shops such as Lee's English Toffee Shop, much like the conditori of Stockholm.

The Tartan Shop discreetly posts in its window a list of names. If you find yours upon it, you're entitled to wear a clan tartan — made up in vest, jacket, or courageously in kilt. Island Weavers displays beautiful hand-woven materials of Canadian wool, in which Canadians take inordinate pride. The young love the Vienna Dirndl Shop on Government Street, importers of Alpine costumes, embroidered cottons and Loden capes.

Antique shops line Fort Street, good for days of browsing among such museum-worthy finds as a cranberry glass punch bowl and ladle with gold overlay, price $500; a muffin warmer dated 1840 by its silversmith, $250; a lovely eighteenth century rosewood cabinet of soft patina, $350; a pair of English coach lanterns, nineteenth century, $125; an eighteenth century rocking horse in such mint condition that its child owner must have been too over-petticoated ever to have climbed to horse, $100; and hold on to your hat, Mary Gregory ladies' wine cups, no larger than an ounce, priced at $30 each.

Cowichan Trading Company at the corner of Government and Johnson Streets has the widest selection of Cowichan Indian sweaters, products of organized endeavour much favored by skiers and steelhead fishermen. Hand-knit of raw wool bleached in the sun, the sweaters are lively with design worked in natural shades of grey and black wool upon white. Lanolin is retained in the wool, giving the sweaters, matching mittens, socks and caps a waterproof quality and soft, slightly oily feel to the fingers. Patterns are inspired by geometric designs on the shells of steamer clams, and by birds and animals native to the island. No two are alike. Recently the trading company was appalled to receive a bundle of sweaters with a jovial elephant worked across the shoulders in black wool. Drastic action — removal of a billboard featuring an elephant from the approach road to the Cowichan Indian Village — put a stop to the disaster.

As Indian carding, spinning and knitting prowess varies, it's a good idea to select and try on with care before making the considerable investment. Sometimes one sleeve is two inches short, or wool has a yellowish tinge from inadequate bleaching. Cowichan Trading handles some 7000 garments a year along with plaques, ceremonial masks, totems, baskets and bentwood boxes, potlatch bowls, moose hide moccasins, Eskimo whalebone and soap stone carvings. In adult sizes sweaters are priced at around forty dollars, fifteen dollars to thirty dollars in children's size range. Ponchos, a new style doubtless inspired by young fashion, are priced at about fifty dollars.

6 BUTCHART GARDENS

Memorial to a great lady.

Next to Inner Harbour, doubtless the most visited spot on Vancouver Island is world-famous Butchart Gardens at Tod Inlet on the Saanich Peninsula. Ten Gray Line lecture tours depart from in front of the Empress Hotel from nine in the morning to eight-thirty in the evening daily (fewer in winter). The story of the gardens' growth is classic Canadian folklore of a woman's will to walk in beauty, and share it with others. The reclaimed limestone quarry, heart of more than 25 acres under intense cultivation, lives in awesome splendor, a vast bowl hewn out of solid rock, containing thousands upon thousands of the earth's choicest flowering shrubs, trees and flowers. It has charmed more than six million strollers on its paths over sixty-five years of gradual development from an ugly hole in the ground to a tapestry of unbelievable beauty. The visitor's guide necessarily is printed in Chinese, French, German, Italian, Japanese, Spanish, Russian, Ukrainian, Danish and Dutch as well as English, for international visitors.

Jennie Butchart was the wife of pioneer cement manufacturer Robert Pim Butchart, who came to western Canada in 1904. He established his business on this 130-acre estate, thirteen miles from downtown Victoria, surrounding a deposit of limestone. When the limestone was exhausted, the pit remained, a gaping hole near the Butcharts' home, Benvenuto.

It offended Jennie's feel for beauty until reclamation of the pit became an obsession. Perhaps it was the natural "Rock Island" looming in the center of the quarry that suggested to her

47

a dramatic setting for a superb alpine garden surrounded by an artificial lake.

Robert Butchart shared his wife's vision to the point of pouring the profits of his business back into the pit. It took years, incalculable tons of top soil, the work of a small army of Chinese helpers, and hundreds of thousands of dollars to transform the insult to the earth into a glorious sunken garden. The Butcharts traveled the world over to bring back rare and exotic bulbs, seeds, shrubs and trees. Holland, the Orient, Alaska and England made the greatest contributions. Sometimes — as with the blue poppy of Tibet — the Butcharts were first to plant precious new seeds in North America.

As the years passed, Jennie Butchart expanded the area to four strikingly different gardens. There are a traditional English rose garden, a formal Italian garden of great elegance and fine statuary, a Japanese garden that contains flowering cherry trees from the Imperial Palace grounds, a tea house and stepping-stone paths over its numerous ponds; and the sunken garden whose walls still flower with blossoms of rare alpine plants tucked into crevices of the rock by Jennie Butchart a half century ago. So lush has grown the basic ivy and Virginia creeper cover of the quarry walls that they have a soft "furred" look, broken now and again by massive rock outcroppings and cascades of forest ferns.

It isn't just one vista, but a contrast of colors, textures, forms and fragrances changing with the seasons and with the constant planting of massed annuals. The old brick kiln chimneys have been left standing in the sunken garden as reminders of its humble origin.

The wonderful gardens now are managed by grandson Ian Ross. He increased public enjoyment by putting in four miles of underground wiring and an illuminated fountain that plays in summers a nightly symphony of changing light and color against the dusky background of deep fir forest. Another innovation is a concert garden where variety shows and Victoria Symphony sunset concerts are attended by crowds on weekday nights of late June to September. A seed house packages rare flower seeds from the garden for sale to visitors.

A good way to see the gardens is that favored by Victorians, who arrive of a summer evening about five o'clock. They stroll for an hour or two in soft afternoon light, have tea or buffet supper at the Floral Restaurant in the old mansion, attend a concert, and then—in full dark—see the gardens once again under hidden lighting effects that turn them into an incredibly beautiful fairyland. The eighty-foot fountain is focal point for night strollers. It should be viewed for at least ten minutes for the full effect of delay-control devices which alter color and pattern.

All road maps indicate the location of the gardens near Brentwood Bay. The approach road is lined with 566 Japanese flowering cherry trees. The entrance fee (there is no extra charge for entertainment or night lighting) is just enough to continue improvement of the estate and maintain its year-round staff of fifty gardeners, enlarged in spring and summer to one hundred fifty. Butchart Gardens are open twelve months of the year, each season bringing its own beauty. If you can't take the crowds (I can't) visit any time after Labor Day to mid-June.

7 WEST OF VICTORIA

The wonder of Botany Bay.

Turn to a map of Vancouver Island and locate Port Renfrew sixty-five miles west of Victoria on Port San Juan, at the mouth of Juan de Fuca Strait, the magnificent body of water separating Canada and the United States. Port Renfrew is at the end of a passable road on the southern island, fairly well known to backpackers as start of the famed Life Saving Trail. On a summer's day of deep minus tides there is uncovered near Port Renfrew a strange inter-tidal wonderland known to marine biologists for its unique sea life for seventy years.

Properly called Botanical Beach, it is familiarly known as Botany Bay. The marine garden extends out into the Pacific about three miles from the small logging and fishing community. Approach from Port Renfrew is via the roughest of deteriorating logging roads. I'm not going to try to tell you how to get there. It's too complicated. If this strange world interests you, write to the Department of Travel Industry, Victoria, and ask for detailed instructions.

Some day when all logging in the area is completed, British Columbia's Parks Branch hopes to provide a passable road to Botany Bay. Uplands bordering the area will be acquired as a buffer zone of protection and public education. Until then Botany Bay is an adventure. Take along a shovel in case you get stuck, drinking water and lunch hamper.

Though sandstone reefs are common enough in the San Juan and Gulf Islands of the Northwest's inland sea, only at Botany Bay has the powerful sculpting action of pounding Pacific waves created so extensive a natural aquarium. Flat shelving sandstone, at low tide more than 500 feet wide, extends for several miles along the Strait and north of San Juan Inlet. Known as the Sooke Formation, it is layered now and again with dark, wave-resistant schist.

Milleniums ago, the ocean bed was compressed into sandstone and raised to form these shelves which have wrecked many a craft. Imbedded throughout the compressed sands are countless rocks of harder substance, ranging in size from thumbnail pebbles to house-sized boulders. Literally stuck in the sandstone like raisins in a cake, they resist the wearing action of waves and tides. As the softer material scours away, these trapped boulders pop out, leaving tidy round potholes behind in countless numbers.

Small rocks wash into the potholes where the churning, swirling, "egg beater" action of the waves scours out huge spherical pools much larger than the original openings indicate. Big potholes are filled with little potholes. Because the holes offer snug housing and security of a sort, they are filled with sea life in waving growth of sea palm and coral algae. It is a marine biologist's and eager child's dream.

The first biological field station on the Pacific coast of Canada and one of the first on the west coast of North America, it was discovered during a 1901 survey. A marine field station was established above the high tide line by the University of Minnesota. On a minus tide the wild beach at the very edge of heavy forest, bound in part by fifty-foot-high cliffs, becomes a masterpiece of pools, basins, caves, thundering blowholes, drowned trees and fantastic underwater life, a vast flat expanse allowing observation of incredible animals at close range. Among them are goose barnacles, many varieties of starfish, edible mussels, sea urchins, beche-de-mers, crabs, anemones, nudibranches, mask limpits, jellyfish, abalones, chitons.

The shelf is doomed — not in our time, but in some thousands of years — because this soft formation cannot forever resist the swirl of tides. Meanwhile it is a rare experience to walk far out on it (with due care for fast-rising returning tide and the safety of little ones), an interloper in a mysterious world, and observe a secret life of unique ecological association usually hidden deep under the sea. Fishing in the Renfrew area, incidentally, is great. Trolling for large coho and chinook salmon, river-fishing for summer-run steelhead, and mooching for halibut all can be arranged at Elliott's Cabins.

You have two choices in return routes. A logging road, lightly used, crosses the southern end of Vancouver Island from Port Renfrew to Trans-Canada No. 1, allowing access to lovely lakes, Fairy Lake with picnicking and swimming beach, and Shawnigan Lake. Its distinctive feature is an extraordinary roller-coaster bridge crossing a precipitous ravine. Hung on cables which dip like a deep hammock, it requires nerve to drive it.

Alternative is Highway No. 14 with occasional views out over the Strait to the Olympic Mountains which will bring you to Sooke Basin. Look southwest to the mouth of the inlet. Here at Whiffen Spit is Sooke Harbour House with rooms overlooking the strait and renowned dining room. Again, deep sea fishing trips can be arranged. Matter of fact, *all* waters of Vancouver Island, fresh and salt, abound in fish. There is no closed season on salmon, trout, steelhead and bass. I know a Victoria businessman who trout fishes a small lake just outside the city limits on his way home from the office! He doesn't hold up dinner, either. If you're in Sooke in July, check the date of All Sooke Day. It's the most professional, exhilarating loggers' sports festival in the Northwest.

8 THE GULFS

A labyrinth of verdant isles.

The islands looming like green stepping stones across Haro Strait and the Strait of Georgia are another world, great areas of them little changed since eighteenth century exploration by British and Spanish sea captains and "the Boston men". Pioneers who settled in the islands, particularly Salt Spring just east of the toe of Vancouver Island, were of a different background from the British colony at the "Port of Camosack"—Victoria.

The big island was named a Crown colony in 1849, but it was owned in entirety by the Hudson's Bay Company. Desiring only settlers of quality and material means, the company placed an exorbitant price on land—one pound per acre. This effectively excluded almost everyone but Hudson's Bay people and colonials bent on living as landed gentry in the raw, new environment. Meanwhile Salt Spring Island, where land might be preempted (homesteaded), during the Civil War attracted emigrants from the United States, many of them blacks fleeing an intolerable life. Their descendants still make up a minority on Salt Spring.

To this day the islands are filled with characters. ALL islands are full of characters, for people who are drawn irresistibly to little private worlds surrounded by sea are individualists unmellowed by the frustrations of ordinary life, people of resolute independence who live on splendid terms with nature. Not the least of the islands' charms is that everyone is expected to be a wee bit peculiar, or even mildly dotty if he has a mind to be and gets fun out of it. His value as neighbor and friend increases right along with his originality of expression. Nobody's up tight.

53

I know an old boy, a real old fashioned English "remittance man" supported by his distant family on condition that he remain out of the British Isles, who for years and years has raided his neighbors' crab pots when his dough is low. Instead of getting indignant about it, the neighbors rather appreciate the zest he adds to local gossip. They do let him know when they expect guests and need the crabs so he can raid somebody else's pot.

Extraordinary things happen to you in the Gulf Islands. Once I happened on a beach oyster barbecue at Booth Bay Resort on Salt Spring and stayed to compete in the main athletic event — a lamb diapering contest! A lady on Galiano Island for years and years has amused the local folk by devoting herself in toto to a fictional work on the life of a seagull. Somehow the joke has lost its savor now that *Jonathan Livingston Seagull* has topped the best sellers for weeks.

The San Juans' prime wit, now sadly deceased, was known far and wide as the Admiral of Coon Island, mostly because he wore a battered yachting cap. His island was right on the route of international ferries crossing between Anacortes in Washington and Sidney on Vancouver Island. The Admiral grew irked at the dead-panned surveillance of passing tourists. Whatever he might be doing — bailing a rowboat, cleaning a fish — there it was again. The look.

So he gave the passing parade something to see. The feats of the Admiral upon a flat rock just off his island now are so wrapped in myth that it is difficult to separate those that are purely imaginary from those shows he actually produced. He is said to have dressed his wife in flowing blonde wig and mermaid's tail, equipped her with ukelele and song, draped her on the rock and hidden his boat away at first sight of the ferry.

Again legend states that he donned runner's pants and a number on his back and furiously pedaled a bicycle around and around the flat rock. On another occasion he gave a lively cocktail party on the rock for all his friends, gussied up in their finest shore clothing, with conspirators to remove all means of transport to the affair. Passengers on the ferries surged to the rail and frantically rolled film into their cameras until Pole Pass was awash with little yellow film boxes.

An island innkeeper until his retirement left his Christmas decorations up year-round. Nightly a great star blazed on his lodge roof and a 200-foot fir tree came to life with hundreds of colored lights, visible from miles at sea. I liked it well enough, but intrigued, asked him why—in July.

"Haw! It lifts the spirits!" he explained, chuckling wickedly with a sound not unlike that of a choking cat and suiting action to words with three fingers of Irish whiskey. The lights were a signal of sorts to boatsmen that the bar was open and functioning.

A prim little woman, a retired schoolteacher, settled on an isolated farm on one of the more northerly islands. Her only companions are two doe-eyed, long-eared Nubian goats of such impeccable manners that it is their mistress' custom to milk them right in her kitchen in rainy weather. The only real problem raised by Emily and Heidi is their need for annual "freshening", the more difficult because the teacher has no car and there are no handy billy goats on the island anyway. A pragmatist, she summons a taxi from the nearest town on Vancouver Island.

Once arrived at the farm with a ferry trip behind and ahead of him, no taxi driver ever has been known to turn down Emily and Heidi. Softly bleating the urgency of their condition in the back seat, the goats ride grandly to their nuptials, their mistress in front with the driver. If ever you hire the particular taxis of the trysts, you'll know them. They smell faintly like sour, wet mops.

Venerable island resorts rapidly are being "modrunized"

and their numbers augmented by lush new lodges that have sprung up in recent years for the yachting and salmon fishing crowd. Here and there lingers an English resort with true turn-of-century flavor, leisurely of service, slightly musty, dusty, lumpy of mattress and beloved of "the regulars" who have returned to them for decades. In such establishments ferociously pink-tinted little-girl prints of Lilibet and Margaret Rose hang on bedroom walls above the sagging brass bedsteads. A photograph of the Prince of Wales in his lettuce days — the late Edward, not Charles — is found in sitting rooms, draped in fishnet held at the corners with little dried starfish above the wheezing player piano.

Notices posted at dining room doors advise ladies that "proper dress", i.e. no slacks or shorts, is expected within. You better believe it. Lobbies are inclined to tasseled lampshades and tottering, stone-deaf desk clerks who do double duty as bellhops, but I've never truly been uncomfortable. There's a certain camaraderie among the patrons that you just don't find in aggressively swimming-pooled, chrome-gleaming modern motels, and now and again the food is superb. Their chief virtue is that they're there, making it possible to know the islands in leisurely fashion.

On the other hand, I'll never forget the famished guests of one such lodge assembled on the beach awaiting low tide with bottles of Worcestshire sauce, ripped off from the dining room sideboard, sticking out of their pants pockets. We all were after oysters, to keep body and soul together. Underway at the lodge was some noisy contretemps with an adamant cook which exploded in hysterical, full-blown decibels every time the swinging kitchen door opened. The wife of the proprietor, her experience at cooking for a dining room full of people severely limited, took over. Unable to multiply her recipes, the dear lady cooked for two, and fed teaspoon portions to us sixteen guests.

56

Sailing away from the island with a fellow sufferer, an elderly British Army officer retired from a career in the "colonies", I was amazed to overhear him instruct his wife:

"Minni, make a note to bring a steamer basket with us next year."

Faint with malnourishment, I managed to scream, "You don't mean you're coming back to the Royal?"

He turned stiffly in my direction, bugged his pale blue eyes, twitched his bristly red and white mustache and announced,

"We ALWAYS spend a fortnight every summer at the Royal."

Lest you think they're all pixilated, herewith a list of island resorts at many of which I've stayed with pleasure, necessarily limited as I have not overnighted on each and every island. In time we ALL become "regulars".

On Salt Spring Island, the Harbour House at Ganges Bay is open all year and has tennis courts and swimming pool. Booth Bay Resort in the Ocean area has pleasant housekeeping cottages right on the water, a private beach for swimming, large clam and oyster beds and nearby trout fishing. There are a dozen others on seventy square mile Salt Spring, most cottage-camp-site-trailer havens, and Mouat Provincial Park at Ganges.

North and South Pender Islands, joined by a narrow bridge across a twisting, noisy channel of fast-moving water, lie in great salmon fishing waters. Favorites of sportsmen are Otter Cove Lodge, near the ferry landing on North Pender, and Bedwell Harbour Resort on South Pender Island. Both have good dining rooms, housekeeping cottages, pools, boat rentals, moorage and charter boat fishing. Beaumont Marine Park for boatsmen is near Bedwell Harbour.

Mayne Island's Mayne Inn is an old-timer, a country home with massive stone fireplace. Mayne's Springwater Lodge in Active Pass, famed for chinook salmon fishing, is beautifully located with great views. Mayne is perhaps too little appreciated.

We became acquainted with a farm family on Mayne Island by stopping by on a spring day to admire a kitchen garden literally bursting out of the soil with exuberant production of lettuce, spinach, radishes, peas—all the early vegetables. Not only was it a thing of beauty, worth seeing on its own, but as the farmer agreed to sell us fresh produce, we visited often. One morning we sprinted up the lane, appalled by the devastation of those exquisite rows. The chickens had got out and descended on the tender plants squawking, gobbling, dust-bathing and scratching with their big yellow feet in a kind of chicken vandal heaven. We rounded the porch at full tilt, sounding the alarm.

Placidly rocking in the sun was the farmer's wife, totally undisturbed by the surrounding havoc.

"It's Mother's Day," she told us, "And all them chickens are mothers." Islanders just have a different way of looking at things.

Long, skinny Galiano Island, sixteen miles by two, the north boundary of Active Pass, has some charmers particularly appropriate to family vacationing. Galiano Lodge at Sturdies Bay on Active Pass, Madrona Lodge on Trincomali Channel, Salishan Resort near the northern end of the island, and nearby Valhalla Campsite (housekeeping cabins and trailer hook-ups) all have devotees who return year after year.

Galiano is singularly interesting among the Gulf Islands. Just off the west shore are the Bellingall Islands, waterfowl sanctuaries. Southern Galiano Island has almost perpendicular cliffs which afford spectacular views out over Active Pass. Covered with rock plants and wild flowers, the bluffs are dominated by the oldest and largest trees on the island.

Roads run the full length of Galiano providing access to resorts, a nine-hole golf course and the rifle range and trap-shooting facilities of the Galiano Rod and Gun Club. A provincial park in a land-locked bay, Montague Harbour Marine Park, is located on Galiano's southwest coast. Facilities include twelve mooring buoys, boat-launching ramp, spring water, campsites, picnic tables and docking needs. These yachtsmen's camps invariably are in fabulously beautiful protected coves that appear to have been fashioned for just this use.

Gabriola Island, reached by car-ferry from Nanaimo, is famous for a dramatic lighthouse at Orlebar Point and the rock fantasy of Malaspina Galleries, sea-pounded caves of sandstone scooped by wind and tides until a six-footer can walk along them without bending his head. Gabriola, which likes to call itself Queen Island of the Gulfs, also has abundant beaches and Gabriola Sands Marine Park. Year-round Silva Bay Resort, Ltd., is a favorite place to stay. Taylor Bay Lodge, near Malaspina Galleries, is especially pleasant for families. There are complete trailer hook-ups here, a salt water pool, tennis courts and lawn games. Surf Lodge is a woodland resort with cottages overlooking Georgia Strait. There's a beautifully decorated lounge with fireplace and a compass room. The swimming pool is sun-warmed salt water, while tennis and archery courts are reached by trails through the woods. Like all spots on Gabriola, the beaches provide shellfish and crabs, the nearby waters good salmon and bottom fishing.

Off Nanaimo, 760-acre Newcastle Island has been set aside in entirety as a marine park. Newcastle has delightful wooded trails with sea views, good swimming beaches, open playing and picnicking fields. There are twenty boat-mooring buoys, camping units, picnic tables and drinking water. Access is by private boat or ferry for pedestrians only—no cars allowed.

Denman and Hornby Islands, reached by car-ferry out of Buckley Bay, are largely agricultural, devoted to pasturage and cows. Rustic accommodations are of the spartan variety with wood stoves, coal oil lamps, cold water and outside plumbing, favored by the beads and sandal set. Denman Island is site of small Fillongley Provincial Park, a pleasant forest and sand beach with camping spaces and picnic area.

Hornby Island's Shingle Spit Resort, at the ferry landing, offers one and two bedroom housekeeping units with propane stoves, fireplaces and showers. Hornby's Seabreeze Guest Farm has a bucolic air—hay rides, home-baked bread, home-grown beef, picnics and beachcombing expeditions. Accommodations are small cabins overlooking the sea, with modern plumbing in a centrally-located building and electric lights. Quiet and kid-oriented, the Farm is American plan only.

Hornby Island Lodge is far and away the most sophisticated of the Denman and Hornby Island resorts, provides outdoor barbecues, saddle horses, fishing boats, tennis courts, outboards for water skiing and hiking trails. The Lodge attracts hunters in fall for the island's grouse, pheasant, quail and deer.

9 THE DISCOVERY ISLANDS

Northern Islands Off Campbell River

My love of them all, the island to which I'd most like to retire
some day, is Quadra, named for Spanish sea captain Juan
Francisco de la Bodega y Quadra. Twenty-eight miles in length,
it is stuck in the mouth of Johnstone Strait, much too far north
to be included in the Gulf Islands which terminate, geograph-
ically speaking, off Nanaimo. The northern islands off Campbell
River generally are lumped together under the title Discovery
Islands, for Discovery Passage. Quadra is reached by frequent
car-ferry across Discovery Passage from downtown Campbell
River. So quick and convenient is this crossing that Quadra
has a surprisingly large population — 2000 permanent residents.
Many of the home-owners at Quathiaski Cove are commuters
to professions and businesses in Campbell River.

Discovery Pass can be pretty hairy in a winter blow, yet the
ferry rarely misses its run right to the heart of Tyee Plaza. The
commuters tell me that a good spraying with icy salt water isn't
a bad way to start the day! And look what they get — isolation
with convenience, life surrounded by such staggering beauty of
nature that it seems a culmination of all the glories of the
Georgia Strait islands.

The northern part of the island, the tiny fishing village of
Granite Bay, can be reached only by rough dirt road, but good
graded gravel will take you to the principal attractions of the
southern island, Yaculta, an Indian fishing village; Cape Mudge
Lighthouse (where the lonely Scots lightkeeper is quite likely
to invite you in to his immaculate quarters for tea and biscuits
followed by a climb to the light), Francisco Point, April Point,

Gowland Harbour, Heriot Bay (from which the little local car-ferry departs for Cortes Island across Sutil Channel), and the most wonderful of all British Columbia Provincial Parks and Campgrounds, that at the trailhead of Rebecca Spit. Beyond Cape Mudge Lighthouse on good trail you'll come across a rare collection of petroglyphs carved in the rock by a prehistoric people many thousand years ago.

Not entirely comprehended or even dated by archaeologists, they are thought to have been the work of a primitive civilization which preceded the Indians. The petroglyphs of Cape Mudge have not been vandalized by modern initial carvers and people who insist on filling the markings with chalk. Those at Nanaimo's Petroglyph Park have been thus desecrated, probably because they are reached so easily.

Once we visited the lighthouse keeper on a day of impenetrable heavy mist. He told us that within minutes the Princess Italia would sail down the Pass, returning from Alaska. We ran out on the rocks to watch for her. Suddenly there loomed a white ghost ship, the sleek Italia, disappearing in the grey dimness as magically as she had appeared. It was a strange feeling, akin to the wonder of the Hesquiat Indians when the Spaniard Juan Josef Perez Hernandez anchored his little corvette Santiago off Estevan Point in 1774.

From any vantage point on Quadra Island, the view on a day when the wind is in the right direction, dispersing the waste products of the giant pulp mill north of Campbell River, is magnificent. Along Discovery Pass, and especially at Cape Mudge, you look deep into the great seven-thousand foot peaks of Strathcona Provincial Park in the center of Vancouver Island, looming snow-covered, serene summits above the trim city of Campbell River. At Francisco Point, view is of wild islands and the massive maelstrom of the Canadian Coast Range. At Heriot Bay and Rebecca Spit, which extends far out into the sea in lonely grandeur, you look into absolute wilderness, the mass of largely unknown mountainous islands at the mouths of Toba and Bute Inlets and at the extreme northern terminus of the Strait of Georgia.

Campgrounds at Rebecca Spit are located at the break where this long, dramatic sandspit extends for some miles to create the quiet, tree-lined coves of Drew Harbour, fabulous marine park with boat moorings on the west side, in contrast to stone beaches of Sutil Channel on the east. Paths and secluded picnic tables extend to the very tip of the point where the sensation of being far out at sea is overwhelming. You're likely to watch the flight of bald eagles, the black fins of a passing pod of killer whales, and the passage of craft ranging from the ferry MV Cortes Queen to fish boats to beautiful yachts. Strangely, you'll have the wooded sandspit all to yourself. Campers are inclined to remain in their immediate area and don't appear to relish these wonderful trails. The campground has fifty units, picnic tables and safe drinking water.

Oyster gathering on low tides is phenomenal. I watched a family staying in a trailer park in Campbell River gather eight gunnysacks of oysters on a minus tide, not exactly cricket because the legal limit is 100 pounds in shell, one gallon shucked, but at least they intended to share them with other trailer-vacationists.

Accommodations at Heriot Bay are Heriot Bay Inn, a pleasant old hotel with dining room and marina; and new Taku Resort, A-frame housekeeping cottages facing Drew Harbour with fishing and boat facilities.

The finest resort in all the islands is secluded April Point Fishing Resort developed by the Peterson family primarily for yachtsmen and tyee salmon fishermen (the big chinooks, weighing up to sixty pounds or even more, taken frequently in the area). Fishing is so good that families spin from the floats for chinooks, cohos and bluebacks. April Point has a thoroughly attractive main lodge right on its three miles of sheltered shoreline on Discovery Passage, with magnificent view of snow-capped mountains of the big island. Surrounding the lodge are completely modern guest houses with sundecks and kitchens, a sauna, and a tremendous salt water swimming pool sun-heated to a summer-constant seventy degrees. Guides, fish boats and motors are available.

April Point Yacht Club is located nearby. In addition to fishing known throughout the world (guests are booked from South America and Europe) there are swimming, waterskiing, sailing, exploring trails through April Point's 200 acres of shorelands, and beachcombing. A custom cannery cares for guests' catch. Cuisine is in keeping with the Petersons' reputation established over the years (top government rating). Considering the sums charged in season for little ma & pa cabins in the islands, April Point rates are not out-of-bounds.

Calendar of fishing is tyee, July through September; coho, July through October; chinooks (also called springs, kings, Quinnauts and when immature, bluebacks), April to September; bluebacks, May through July; rainbow and cutthroat trout freshwater lake fishing, all year; and steelhead, December through April. Pick up a copy of Tidal Waters Sport Fishing Guide, detailing bag limits and gear restrictions, at any tourist bureau or resort.

The sheer size of chinook salmon caught on rod and line every year in any number of salt water areas of British Columbia is staggering. Most giant chinooks — tyees — are caught by trolling as the fish near the spawning rivers. The current record for tidal waters is held by Rivers Inlet on the mainland, where an eighty-two pounder was taken in 1952. No year goes by without catches of over sixty pounds.

Cohos, or silvers, offer a faster sport. They are taken trolling in salt water and as they are feeding actively, will rise to a large fly fished just under the surface. Many fly fishermen use five or six ounce rods, which give cohos a chance to put on a dazzling, head-shaking, tail-hopping performance. Feeding salmon are caught also by casting with strips or herring plugs, worked adroitly through the water. Artificial trolling lures, especially in the evening, have their believers. Ask the guides or locals. They know what is producing, and where.

Cortes Island accommodations are limited to Manson's Landing, where a country store is surrounded by rustic housekeeping cabins with oil stoves, cold water and central showers.

You'll get an occasional whiff of the Crown Zellerbach pulp mill at Duncan Bay, and see its smudge across the heavens, even in the Discovery Islands. Great efforts are underway to abate the nuisance. Until the answer is found, you'll just have to get used to an occasional kind of rotten egg-outhouse reminder in the air that Vancouver Island contains fifteen percent volume of all British Columbia's mature timber and the majority of its pulp capacity. Forest products industries are way out front as leading employment of the island. Port Alice at the far reaches of Quatsino Sound at the north end of the island had the only pulp mill prior to World War II. The industry is off and running now with five large new mills at Crofton (pulp and newsprint), Harmac near Nanaimo (pulp), Duncan Bay near Campbell River (pulp, newsprint and kraft paper), Port Alberni (pulp, newsprint and kraft paper) and Gold River (pulp). The big logging operators are MacMillan and Bloedel Company, BC Forest Products and Rayonier of Canada, Ltd. Islanders live from trees, tourists and fish, in that order.

10 UP-ISLAND

The communities of Island Highway.

Island Highway swings north of Victoria over the Malahat, a considerable mountain whose early road in my childhood was considered fit only for the foolhardy, even by Canadians, those intrepid drivers. Re-engineered at least twice since then, it now rises to a pleasant, easy, 1200-foot summit with spectacular view down Saanich Inlet to Islands and the distant mainland. Approaching Duncan, the first largish town, watch for Koksilah's Canoe Store and turn-off east to the Indian village at the mouth of the Cowichan River. The Cowichan is one of the great rivers of Vancouver Island, famed for its summer and winter runs of steelhead, sea-run rainbow trout which grow to thirty pounds.

II COWICHAN INDIAN COUNTRY

Artistic ability leads to proud independence.

On Tzouhalem Road you'll see the still-beautiful shell of the first stone church built on Vancouver Island, known to the Indians as Clemclemaluts Catholic Mission Church, to whites as Old Stone Church or the Butter Church. It was built by Father Rondeaults who came ashore by canoe in Cowichan Bay in 1852 to work with the Indians. The priest contracted with one Mr. Williams, a white, to supply material which could not be procured on the site and supervise construction by volunteer Indian parishioners. Soon all funds were gone, but Father Rondeaults had two cows. He churned their cream into butter and sold it to settlers of the area to pay Williams and keep the project going. The church was consecrated in 1870 by Bishop Modeste Demers.

The village of Comiaken surrounds the church. With any luck at all, you'll see and talk with Cowichan Indian knitters working out-of-doors. In the 1880s, Shetland Islanders settled in the Cowichan River Valley, bringing with them domestic sheep. Among them was a brisk little Scotswoman who observed the excellence of Indian weaving. Long before white men came, Indians gathered the wool of mountain goats, a handful at a time, and wove it into blankets and mats.

The Scotswoman, whose identity has not been retained, shared her fleece and taught Indian weavers a white woman's art — the knitting of warm sweaters and socks. The Indians devised their own ingenious instruments for carding the wool and spinning it into thick, soft yarn, using altered foot-pedal sewing machines. The art soon spread to other tribes along a

A Cowichan Indian hanging washed fleece in the sun to bleach, first step in the creation of the Indians' beautiful and practical sweaters.

68

seventy-mile stretch of the eastern shoreline, to the Chemainus, Nanaimos, Quamichans, Songhees and Saanich. Vancouver Island sportsmen became aware of the wonderful garments and soon they began to appear at sporting events.

Norman Lougheed, member of an old Victoria family who has worn Indian sweaters since boyhood, believed that the Cowichans' obvious artistic ability could be their means of attaining economic security. He began to distribute the sweaters, establishing the Cowichan Trading Post and shipping garments to sports outlets, Hudson's Bay posts in the north country and ski shops. Year by year he raised Indian production without altering methods or sacrificing the quality and originality of the work.

Lougheed's company purchases thousands of pounds of raw wool, distributing it to knitters in ten-pound bags — seven of white, three pounds of precious black which is used in the pattern and spun with white for shades of grey. Only three or four pounds end up in a sweater, the fleece of longest, silkiest fiber. Yarns are washed but never dyed as the process would remove oils valued as water repellant. All true Cowichan sweaters are in natural white, grey and black.

About one thousand women are experts, working as consistently as they wish. Most of the price of the finished garment goes to the knitter. The trading company takes a share for sales and distribution, and bookkeeping totally incomprehensible to an outsider. Arrangements with knitters involve complicated barters for payments on television sets, washing machines, radios and cars. Sometimes a debt for bailing a frisky husband out of the pokey is listed as "one sweater due". All wool is purchased by the villagers on credit. Even cash is extended to families with sickness or other emergency. Says Lougheed,

"We understand all this because we're dealing with friends. It has taken years of fair play and patience to reach the point where we work together smoothly. The Cowichans are among the world's great natural artists. I'm their most enthusiastic fan. I've bought lovely sweaters from eight-year-old girls and equally handsome ones from grannies in their nineties. It just wells out of them as if the natural medium for the expression of the beauty they feel is ten-inch knitting needles and bags of fleece."

Chief dividend has been proud independence for these gifted people.

A Cowichan Indian grandmother examines her soft, thick yarn spun from raw wool.

12 THE FOREST MUSEUM

A unique outdoor museum—the story of the evolution of forest industries.

One mile north of Duncan watch for the Cowichan Valley Forest Museum, unique outdoor museum where youngsters are encouraged to scramble all over the exhibits. The museum's curators figure that if its historic logging machinery was stout enough to survive decades of service in Northwest timber country, and years of exposure to the elements, it won't be damaged by adventurous children playing loggers and engineers.

Non-profit, the Forest Museum is dedicated to telling the story of man and the woods through the collection of Gerald Wellburn. A logger, Wellburn viewed first-hand the evolution of forest industries from a largely hand-operated enterprise to the highly mechanized methods of today. This born collector believed that unless historical equipment was restored and displayed, no visible record would remain of a vital century in Vancouver Island industry. Besides he was a puffer-belly railroad and steam engine buff.

Surrounding towns and forest industry incorporated the museum to display the collection, acquiring for it the forty-acre site on the shores of Somenos Lake. It took months to move the rolling stock, antique machinery of steam logging, a water wheel, old log bunk houses and railway station, donkey engines, ancient trucks, wagons and buggies to the park-like grounds. A narrow-gauge, mile-long railway circles the area. As in the early days of logging, Chinese track gangs laid the old steel tracks and built a 300-foot trestle to carry trains over an arm of the lake.

*The non-profit Forest Museum, one mile north of
Duncan, is an unique outdoor collection of
historic puffer-belly locomotives, rolling stock,
antique steam machinery of early logging days,
donkey engines, ancient trucks and buggies
surrounded by the mile-long Cowichan Valley
Railway. A particular delight of a visit to the
Forest Museum is a ride on the railway, which
crosses a cove of Somenos Lake on a 300-foot
wooden trestle. That's the porch of a 19th century
loggers' bunkhouse in the foreground.*

Heavy equipment, whole logs and sections of trees are placed in the open around the park. Final touch was the construction of a massive log museum to house a great variety of small objects and tools used in turn-of-century logging. A prime exhibit is one of the most complete photographic records in existence of early logging and sawmilling methods. The oldest fir tree in the world is represented by an immense section cut from the trunk of an island Douglas fir. It was felled at the approximate age of 1340 years.

Children are torn between the tremendous excitement of riding the rails and the joys of operating a short-line pump car, the kind with handles you push up and down to get the car humping along at a good clip. The museum is open daily from mid-May through September, from ten in the morning to five-thirty in the evening. Modest fees are used for maintenance and expansion. Admission includes rides on the train.

Just north of Ladysmith, like Chemainus a sawmill town, Ivy Green Provincial Park offers camping, abundant picnic tables and a pleasant beach much liked by waterfowl and children. Just beyond Ivy Green a secondary paved road leads east to a dramatic outcropping of rock on Stuart Channel called Yellow Point, an exceptionally beautiful region of forest, sea coves and glacier-polished rock. There's a venerable log lodge here with rustic cabins secluded in the surrounding 200 acres of parklands, saltwater swimming pool, tennis courts, boats and trails. Yellow Point Lodge enjoys a reputation for good food, served barbecue fashion and in the kind of dining room in which the waitresses are grandmothers with a kindly interest in guests' appetites and preferences. Almost all guests are repeaters.

13 NANAIMO

Prime entry port for central Vancouver Island.

A loop road will take you to Nanaimo and Departure Bay, a far cry from the grimy company coal mining town of my childhood. Nanaimo now is prime entry point for all of central Vancouver Island with abundant shipping and ferry connections with Vancouver. The city's exotic name is an adaptation of Coast Salish "Sne-ney-mo", meaning meeting place. In recent years Nanaimo has become a considerable tourist center for exploration up-island, and thus has large numbers of spanking new motels. Coal mining is long gone, the mines shutting down for good in 1945.

Personal favorite for overnighting is the Malaspina Hotel on Front Street, especially a room high up overlooking busy Nanaimo Harbour and out toward Gabriola and Newcastle Islands.

There's good trout fishing in the Nanaimo Lakes and the great salmon fishing to be expected off the mouth of a major river. A seventy-two-par, eighteen-hole golf course and that lovely provincial park on 760-acre Newcastle Island in Nanaimo Harbour, reached by pedestrian-only ferry from the city's waterfront, are visitor favorites. Nanaimo is not a romantic city, but it has saved a handsome reminder of its history, the Bastion.

This octagonal building of great logs was heart of a small fort erected by the Hudson's Bay Company in 1853 to protect the company's coal miners from occasional Indian troubles. The Bastion, now moved from its original site to Front Street in the center of the city overlooking the harbour, still is flanked by its two six-pounders. Apparently the only use ever found for these cannons was salutes to visiting VIPs, for certainly no Indian ever bit the dust with ball fired from these old timers. When need for a fort ran its course, the Bastion was used as a jail. It now houses a pretty good museum.

Unfortunately, goons have done a deal of damage to the petroglyphs in a small park just south of Nanaimo, carving initials in them, filling the ancient indentations with crayon and chalk to make them visible for photographs. The only indication of a mysterious people who inhabited Vancouver Island thousands of years before the Indians, petroglyphs without embellishment can be seen in less accessible spots. One of the finest locations is just beyond Cape Mudge Lighthouse on Quadra Island. Others are the cliffs of Nitinat Lake near Clo-oose on the west coast, Sproat Lake, in the Sooke Harbour area and at Schooner Cove of Pacific Rim National Park.

Each July Nanaimo hosts the gayest of crowds at its four-day Bathtub Regatta, an absolutely wacky series of celebrations climaxed when hundreds of sailors take off across Georgia Strait for Vancouver in tiny, high-powered craft in the form of bathtubs. Now Georgia Strait at this point is an open thirty-six-mile-wide body of water given to occasional wild fury, strong tides and williwaws. Thus the little one-man tubs are accompanied by a fleet of observers ready and able to effect rescues. Contestants come from all over Canada, some from the United States. Winning times run around two hours.

In the last week of August Nanaimo hosts another major aquatic event, the Protection Island Swim about a half mile across Nanaimo Harbour. A couple hundred athletes compete annually. Far fewer turn out for the Polar Bear Swim on Boxing Day, the first weekday after Christmas.

Between Nanaimo and Courtenay the Island Highway runs right along the water, giving access to a parade of lovely coves and warm, shallow swimming beaches with the smell of wood-smoke in the air and the music of children's laughter. A round-up includes Departure Bay, Nanoose Bay, Parksville, Qualicum Beach, Bowser, Mud Bay, Fanny Bay and Buckley Bay. Parksville is turn-off point for the twenty-nine-mile drive to Port Alberni at the headwaters of Alberni Inlet and one of the top adventures awaiting visitors to Vancouver Island — voyage aboard the freight, mail and passenger ship Lady Rose to Bamfield and Ucluelet at the mouth of the west coast's wild Barkley Sound. This trip will be detailed in the section devoted to exploring the west coast.

Trailer parks, tenting areas, little clusters of family beach cottages, many decidedly the worse for decades of wear; and a few lodges with a touch of European glamour line the east coast span north of Nanaimo.

The best known beach is Qualicum, for many years one of the major resort centers of British Columbia. A sandy beach here spreads in a wide curve for more than two miles. A public golf course looks directly out over Georgia Strait to Lasqueti and Texada Islands. Two splendid provincial parks and campgrounds, Englishman River and Little Qualicum Falls, are located a few miles inland, each with a generous one hundred camping units, abundant picnic tables, piped water and heavily forested trails to spectacular waterfalls.

The George Inn, overlooking the golf course and inland sea, is a thoroughly lush place to stay, very English Tudor with canopied beds, Finnish sauna, heated indoor pool and wassail room. Also good is the Shoreline Motor Inn, offering one and two bedroom housekeeping units and pleasant dining room.

The Qualicum Beach Chamber of Commerce will steer you to salmon fishing guides and boats at French Creek Marina, a government boat basin. There's great freshwater fishing at Horne and Spider Lakes on Qualicum River and at Cameron and Great Central Lakes reached from the Port Alberni Highway, No. 4.

Just south of Parksville is new Rathtrevor Beach Provincial Park on a sandy beach, warm and shallow for safe swimming. Rathtrevor has one hundred campsites, a large picnic area and all the comforts. Though less celebrated than Qualicum, the beaches of the Parksville region are among the best on the east coast. Island Hall Hotel is located on such a beach. A huge hotel by up-island standards, Island Hall has made an institution of its daily noontime smorgasbord. Guests are pampered with an indoor pool and turbo-jet pool and tennis courts. It's quite a place, a decided improvement over a paper-thin-walled Parksville hotel at which we stayed one snowy December night.

Shortly after our arrival an impassioned pair settled into the room next door. Immediately it became apparent that anything noisier on our part than muffled breathing would embarrass them cruelly, and that the tryst was clandestine. All innocently we were helpless ear-witnesses of a marathon outpouring of "How do I love thee? Let me count the ways . . .", an agony of lovemaking strictly rated X. By morning we were perishing with vulgar curiosity to catch a glimpse of them. We crept into our clothes and descended for breakfast, expecting at the very least Madame Bovary and Casanova, Lola Montez and Rhett Butler, a gorgeous star-crossed pair trapped by monstrous fate.

Soon there descended a plain brown mouse of a middle-aged woman, shapeless as a sack of potatoes, accompanied by a scrawny lover who would offer no competition in physical charms on his best day to Woody Allen.

As my mother used to reassure her daughters when we were in our timorous teens, there's somebody for everyone.

14 FORBIDDEN PLATEAU

Indian legend gave this area its sinister name.

Courtenay and Comox, in a handsome agricultural valley, are east coast takeoff points for Forbidden Plateau and mountainous Strathcona Park. The ski area of Forbidden Plateau, functioning from December through March with five lifts and a day lodge, is twelve miles from Courtenay over winding gravel road. Unpleasantly dusty in summer, it is worth driving on a day of great clarity for a panoramic view over a vast chunk of the world, Georgia Strait, Islands, the great mountains of the Canadian Coast Range on the mainland. Above the ski lodge is the trailhead of routes leading deep into Strathcona over a high plateau covered with wildflowers in early summer, dotted with gemlike tarns of crystal purity.

Indian legend gave Forbidden Plateau its sinister name. Before the white man came, the central part of Vancouver Island was occupied by two warring tribes, the Cowichans and the Komoux. A medicine man of the Komoux discovered the great plateau on the shoulder of Mount Albert Edward. When once again the war canoes of the Cowichans were seen making their way north to raid the Komoux, all women and children were sent up to safety on the plateau.

A great battle raged, but at last the Cowichans were repulsed. The victorious Komoux ascended the plateau to bring down their families. No trace of them ever was found in weeks of searching, and no hint of their fate. The Indians came to believe that their women and children had been carried off by a race of giants who lived in the ice caves of Mount Albert Edward. To this day the plateau is "forbidden" to members of the Komoux tribe.

Fourteen miles north of Courtenay Island Highway approaches the coast again at Miracle Beach, probably the most popular provincial park on Vancouver Island, incorporating 326 acres of beach and forest. When the tide is out, the beach is an eye-popping expanse filled with tidal pools, so extensive that campers in 182 units make little impression upon it. A special lure of Miracle Beach is the nature house with aquariums and other displays, and first-rate guided nature walks designed to aid tyro nature students. It's a great family beach, safe, its waters shallow a long way out, and warm. Camping units are so arranged that each family enjoys privacy. Canadians pay a deal of attention to this factor.

*Pebble beaches along the east shore of
Rebecca Spit on Quadra Island overlook a
magnificent wilderness, the mass of largely
unknown islands rising to mountainous heights in
the extreme northern waters of Georgia Strait.
The little inter-island ferry Cortes Queen,
en route from Whaletown on Cortes Island to
Heriot Bay on Quadra Island, can be
seen in the distance.*

15 CAMPBELL RIVER

Center of the Tyee Madness.

The big center up-island is Campbell River, much of its growth so recent that the town has a spanking new look, a fresh, vital air especially apparent in Tyee Plaza and anywhere along the waterfront. There's a frontier feel too, for north of Campbell River is a different world, a wilderness cut off sharply from the gentle south island by closed logging areas. Most of the northern one-third of Vancouver Island is Crown land under lease to logging companies which restrict public access over their rough private roads. Campbell River is the gateway to a tremendous area so wild that hunters seeks its cougar, deer and bear, bald eagles fly its skies, and tyee salmon of incredible size come home to its rushing rivers to spawn.

All this makes the creature comforts of Campbell River, fine hotels like Discovery Inn, Haida Inn, Dolphins Resort and Painter's Lodge, all the more astonishing. Campbell River has pizzaz, a rare combo of sophistication, an untamed world to explore, and an incomparable location at the northern end of the inland sea, Georgia Strait.

Personal favorite among Campbell River's many pleasant places to stay is Discovery Inn. The dear people here know that I love a room high up, facing Discovery Passage. At twilight around ten o'clock on a summer night, the lights come on across the Pass at Quathiaski Cove on Quadra Island. Sports fishermen make their way back to the many boat ramps and marinas, while the commercial gillnetters set out for the night's work. The Quadra Queen blazes like a mobile lighted birthday cake and a

81

long V flight of Canada geese is silhouetted against a darkening sky.

The Discovery Inn is one of the Delta Hotels which on Vancouver Island can be found in the most unexpected places, havens of excellence in the wilds at Gold River (Gold River Chalet), Tahsis (Tahsis Chalet) and Rumble Beach "instant town" near Port Alice (Quatsino Chalet). These three were constructed to care for VIPs of the lumber and pulp mills including Princess Margaretha of Denmark (Danish royalty has interests in the Tahsis Company of Muchalat Inlet and Tahsis Arm of Nootka Sound). But they welcome tourists, hunters and fishermen too. There's something far out about a heated hotel swimming pool at Rumble Beach deep in the reaches of Neuroutsos Inlet of Quatsino Sound, reached by air service from Vancouver or Campbell River.

There are two provincial park campgrounds in the Campbell River area, Elk Falls four miles up the river, and Morton Lake, seventeen miles northwest of town via the highway to Kelsey Bay and a gravel access road, good for freshwater swimming, fishing and boating.

Prime attraction is the legendary salmon fishing which has induced town boosters to refer to Campbell River as "the sport fishing capital of the world". Its normal population of about 10,000 jumps to 30,000 at the height of the salmon fishing season. The big trailer parks at Tyee Spit are filled to capacity from the first of April, steelhead season in the rivers and the beginning of blueback and chinook runs in the salt chuck, to October, coho season. Painter's Lodge has been the center of the tyee madness ever since Campbell River was no more than a little fishing village way up there in the wilds.

This tyee business should be explained. Out on Tyee Spit at the mouth of the river, just north of the business section of town, is the Tyee Club, an elite organization which you can join

82

Multiple little islets, wooded as thick as cat's fur,
loom out of the early-morning mists of
Johnstone Strait to add to the enchantment of this
voyage abroad the Island Princess.

in just one way. You have to land under Tyee Club regulations a fighting chinook salmon, a tyee (Indian for Chief) that scales over thirty pounds. Then you're eligible for a coveted trophy button and may get your picture posted in Painter's lobby along with those of Bing Crosby, Bob Hope and other members of this most exclusive club on the continent.

Once the ladies at Painter's were fishing widows, patiently seated under the trees working at needlepoint while their harried husbands went through the agony-ecstasy of sixteen-hour days trolling through Discovery Pass for an over-thirty. Now they're out fishing with their husbands, every bit as mesmerized by the tyee mystique.

The Tyee Club sternly would bar me at the door. I don't care what I catch, or how big it is, as long as I can fillet it at once and take off for the nearest picnic grounds. Sauteed almost while still wiggling in a disgraceful amount of butter, seasoned with fresh ground pepper and salt, all fish is marvelous. Even the lowly ling cod, so ugly it should be ashamed of itself, is as good as lobster tail prepared this way. If your fish-eating experience has been confined to those supermarket frozen, fried, plastic "sticks", you have an eating experience in store.

There's a custom cannery interesting to visit for its kooky personal can labels. Years ago, before British Columbia placed a possession limit on salmon (two single day four-salmon bag limits per fisherman) I found the people of Campbell River seething with indignation over the annual invasion of a huge Texas family. Completely self-contained down to the last bean, they settled their trailers and boats into a then-free public campground and got out the Mason jars and Burpee canner. To increase bag limits, everyone fished down to the littlest kid, and all helped put up the salmon far into the night. Naturally they were amazingly lucky. When the last jar was filled the trailers sagged out of the camp, loaded with a year's supply of Discovery

84

Pass salmon. They managed never to spend a nickel in town. Fish hogs would have trouble crossing the border with such loot nowadays.

Campbell River has other interests, including a sporty golf course. The museum in the Centennial Building houses an excellent collection of Coast Indian artifacts and historical treasures including a first edition of Captain George Vancouver's journal, published in 1798, with an account of the first European ship's passage clear around Vancouver Island.

Mitlenatch Island Provincial Park, a fascinating bird sanctuary twelve miles from Campbell River, is accessible by charter boat. In winter there's helicopter skiing in Strathcona's vast snowfields. Ripple Rock Lookout, up the highway, provides a panoramic view of Seymour Narrows, scene of the once dangerous rock which took a terrible toll of men and boats, — 150 wrecks, at least twenty of them major, and 174 lives. Ripple Rock long since was cleared away by the largest man-made non-nuclear blast ever attempted, but the Narrows still are exciting watching for incoming tidal floods south and the outgoing ebb.

Campbell River is takeoff point over sixty-five miles of paved highway for Strathcona Park, instant town Gold River and the headwaters of Muchalat Inlet of Nootka Sound. The dock at Muchalat is home port of Captain Esson Young's celebrated Uchuck III, freight-passenger-mail boat which serves all the floating logging camps, Indian fishing villages, sawmill towns and sports camps of Nootka Sound from Zeballos to Captain Cook's Friendly Cove. These incomparable voyages, wild and wonderful, will be detailed in the section on the west coast.

16 ON TO KELSEY BAY AND THE INSIDE PASSAGE

Kelsey Bay—the southern port for two terrific car-ferry trips.

North of Seymour Narrows, the highway turns inland to avoid the mountainous coast along Johnstone Strait, continuing fifty miles to the company logging town and docks at Kelsey Bay. It will give you a fine taste of northern Vancouver Island especially as you cross great rivers, the Salmon and White, and look out over lakes, logging operations, and an immense forested interior valley bound by the massif of 7095-foot Victoria Peak. Sayward, near Kelsey Bay, has a few accommodations on the Salmon River. On the dock at Kelsey Bay there's a tiny grocery store. Currently absolute end of paved Island Highway, Kelsey Bay will lose this distinction when the road is extended north to Beaver Cove in the late seventies and connection is made with the paved road extending from Beaver Cove to Port Hardy, "metropolis" of northern Vancouver Island.

The great thing about Kelsey Bay is that it is southern port for two widely varying but absolutely terrific car-ferry trips up the Inside Passage. Hopefully you remember mention of them in the chapter on Seagoing Highways, Vancouver Island's ferry system. The luxury ship is the Queen of Prince Rupert, bound 330 miles north for connection with Alaska ferries at British Columbia's northernmost large port, Prince Rupert.

The workaday ship is the Island Princess, bound north through one of the loveliest sections of the Inside Passage for Beaver Cove on Vancouver Island, Alert Bay on Cormorant Island and Sointula on Malcolm Island at the mouth of Queen Charlotte Strait. This five and one-half to six hour run through sheltered waters of overwhelming grandeur at the pokey pace of nine miles per hour is the ideal way to sail Johnstone Strait. On a

86

long summer day of light lingering far into the evening, you don't miss a thing, not a seiner setting its net, not a family of playful killer whales or rare trumpeter swans making for an isolated lake of the interior.

I fight with the Queen of Prince Rupert whose twenty-hour schedule calls for departures from both her termini in the afternoon so that much of this glorious world is passed in the night. Besides, her cruising speed is eighteen knots, too fast to absorb it all. I'm in love with this wondrous land, forever greedy to see more, learn more.

"Why don't you run out of steaks, break down, stop, visit ports en route, loaf along?" I asked a ferries system official.

"The Queen is an extension of the highways, intended for rapid transportation over a salt chuck freeway. You're taking the wrong attitude. It's transportation in luxury, not a Haida war canoe."

I get even in a way. I go in the long days of the year and stay awake through the luminous far-north nights, perched on a stool on the captain's bridge, absolutely hypnotized by the phosphorescent swirl of current, the shadows of trees and islands on the water, the thunder of waterfalls white against the blackness of shore, the sharp smell of the night's wet salt air, the pale ghosts of following gulls and rifle-sharp plop of giant fish. Yes, the Queen has staterooms. I use mine for brushing teeth and taking a shower.

The graceful white Queen departs each terminal on alternate days from early May to late September, in winter sails northbound on Tuesdays and Thursdays, southbound Wednesdays and Saturdays. One way for car and driver in summer is sixty dollars (berths and meals not included), in winter forty-five dollars with saving on a round-trip ticket. As with all the big ferries, the Queen is met by motor coach service for foot passengers.

17 THE PLAYTEX PRINCESS

The endearing lifeline of the north coast.

She's really the Island Princess, this catamaran personality kid who waddles sedately every day between Kelsey Bay and her northern ports. She came into her popular name when the B. C. Coast Ferries system stretched her three ways to accommodate her increasing popularity. Lengthened fifty feet, widened thirty feet, raised ten feet in height, she now can take up to fifty cars and two hundred ninety in passengers and crew. For all her million-dollar burgeoning she still retains her original power plant, two doughty Rolls Royce truck engines!

The "regulars", off-duty loggers, iron miners from Port Hardy, bored housewives bound for "town" at Campbell River, grow right provoked at her pace, but for vacationists it couldn't be better. You won't believe this, but one-way cost of the trip from Kelsey Bay to Alert Bay — one hundred eleven miles round trip, a great chunk of the Inside Passage, quite possibly the most beautiful cruise in the northern hemisphere — is just four dollars for a walk-on passenger!

Because its customers are something special, people of the frontier, so is the extraordinary milieu of the Island Princess. Sailing north I noticed a pretty, panicky girl in her late teens, bound for a job in communications at Port Alice. Now that the die was cast, she was terrified at the prospect of life in a wilderness community she couldn't even locate on the map. Taking her in tow, I headed for Captain Stan Fike's wheelhouse.

Gently he informed her that she'd be a sensation in Port Alice, a town in which sweet young things with blue, blue eyes are in short supply. She looked dubious until he made a bet with her.

"A dollar says that next time you sail the Island Princess you'll be engaged to a fine man."

A sentimental lady of Sointula, moving down island, discovered that she couldn't bear separation from her cow, now in the last lap of pregnancy. Explaining the problem to the Playtex' captain, she worked out logistics problems beautifully, purchasing tickets for enceinte cow and self, arranging for a belly sling to lift the cow on and off. Captain Fike still needed approval from the home office, which came through speedily with the ambience for which the ship is renowned:

"If pregnant cow cooperative, have no objection."

On another occasion a lady of a logging camp suddenly was called to Toronto by family crisis. She left by plane, weeping at abandoning her eight goats. She did, however, inform the Island Princess of their lonely plight. The crew located an interim keeper for them at another port. A deckhand rounded them up, tying them in long line with a spare ship's rope. He then led them down a gangplank and right through the passenger lounge to an enclosure prepared on deck. They sailed placidly to their new home, causing far less trouble than occasional rambunctious fishermen.

One such Indian threesome started an all-out brawl on the ferry one day. Reporting the incident to the home office, the captain explained, "They were admonished in three languages, English, Coast Salish and profane."

An Indian elder of a remote island, flush from a good season's fishing, made the down payment on a luxury automobile at a mainland city, and paid to have it delivered by barge. As his island has no roads, the automobile was purely one-upmanship, a declaration of superior status. Seated grandly in it in his front yard, the proud owner gained enormous prestige with his peers.

Long before the first monthly payment was due, he had gifted friends and relatives with everything that could be removed. Tires became a fishing boat's fenders, seats household furniture, steering wheel a children's rolling hoop and so on, until the car was a mere shadow of its grand and shiny self. Demands for further payment were ignored. He had paid, hadn't he? After months of futile form letters, the Island Princess carried north a string of adjustors, insurance and otherwise, credit men and such bent on reclamation of the vehicle or resolution of the debt.

In time the agency came to accept the Island Princess' considered opinion that the battered shell was not worth the fee to barge it south. As far as I know, its owner still sits in its fading grandeur, numero uno elder of the village.

North-bound passengers may debark at Beaver Cove and drive or ride Vancouver Island Coach Lines as far as Port Hardy, a town with more feel of transient logging camp than ocean port. Some of its company houses, built on logs for floating to other locales, still are occupied. There's a campground, Cheslakees Campsite, en route near the mouth of the Nimpkish River on Broughton Strait. This is end of the line for the coaches, which do not drive the road to the old whaling town of Coal Harbour, restricted roads to Holberg, remote Winter Harbour or Port Alice. Where Island Coach Lines won't drive, I don't drive. I'm content to fly in to Port Alice and there charter a local boat for exploration of Quatsino Sound.

Travel over restricted roads is subject to complete closure at any time deemed advisable for dangerous fire weather, accelerated logging truck use, or other hazard. You can get stuck in more ways than one. Expect pioneer roads, narrow, dirt and rough. Restrictions are maintained rigidly for the safety of all: no public travel from seven in the morning to five-thirty in the afternoon on logging work days, when a meeting with a logging

90

truck could be pure disaster for both. Rayonier of Canada will supply up-to-date information, maps and permits from their offices at 1111 West Georgia Street in Vancouver, and at Port McNeill, Jeune Landing, Port Alice and Holberg. For travel over the restricted Port Hardy Forest Development Road obtain your permit from the Forest Ranger at Port Hardy. MacMillan Bloedel private roads are controlled from their office in Port Hardy.

If this seems vaguely inhospitable, know that all logging trucks are in constant radio communication with controls and one another. They don't meet unexpectedly on blind curves. There's no practical way of checking whereabouts of a stray tourist playing automotive Russian roulette.

The Island Princess stops also at Sointula, populated by the Finnish descendants of a long-gone Utopia. At turn-of-century a Finnish political refugee founded the settlement called "place of harmony" on 20,000 acres granted by the British Columbia government. Most of these pioneers, living together in community halls, were intellectuals completely unsuited to the hard life. They struggled bravely to find a way to support their socialistic ideals, submitting bids on bridge construction in North Vancouver.

The bids were far too low, exhausting their limited funds. Their founder abandoned the community to its fate. Until very recent times, the only language spoken at Sointula was Finnish, but now the children are ferried across the steamer route every day to schools at Port McNeill, where they have learned English and the ways of the Twentieth Century. Outsiders are made welcome at Sointula's little Ship's Inn. If you plan to overnight at Sointula, end of the run for the Island Princess, reservations are advised. Life still is very simple on Malcolm Island. The men fish or find work in the woods.

18 ALERT BAY

Kwakiutl fishing village on the Island Princess' run.

Alert Bay is my choice for the nightly layover on the Island Princess' run, especially for the splendid display of Kwakiutl totems in the Indian cemetery. An eastern journalist once wrote of Alert Bay that it is "sinister", its Indian inhabitants "frightening".

I find this absolute hogwash.

I've been stuck in Alert Bay, sitting out walking-gull fogs, on several small seaplane flights to northern points, and have thoroughly enjoyed its magnificent scenic beauty when I could glimpse it through the fog. Other pleasures are walks on the beaches and scant roads of the three-mile-long island, activity at its busy harbour, visits to its salmon canneries, and in June, its Indian Sports Day and Salmon Barbecue.

True, it is an Indian town, with a very long history of human habitation. But only an easterner could find this "sinister". There are two hotels, best avoided on Saturday nights when the first-floor pubs are rocking. Alert Bay citizens are pretty frank about Saturday nights. "The drunks may keep you awake." Nimpkish Hotel, Box 49, Alert Bay, has eight double rooms with private baths. Reservations are a good idea.

You'll get used to beat-up Indian-owned taxis in some remote areas—not Alert Bay, where they're clean as a whistle and come on the run. Others are transportation only, often redolent of fish, animals and choking clouds of dust rising from the interior. Drivers are stimulating in the Barney Oldfield tradition, and right hep on local attractions and gossip. They're especially well versed on fishing and hunting, and who got in his cups last night, what altercation ensued, and the outcome.

19 LONELY NORTHERN ISLAND

Exploring this virgin country is far removed from the usual tourist experience.

A trail is the only route to the extreme northwest end of Vancouver Island, reaching remnants of the isolated Danish settlement at Cape Scott, William Lake, San Josef Bay and Holberg. Every once in a while an adventurous mountaineering club of the Northwest organizes a week-long backpack over this route, in part for its rugged beauty and the fishing, more for its sad history. Cape Scott and the offshore rocks, Lanz, Cox, Triangle, Sartine and Beresford Islands, thrust their wicked jagged teeth out into the open Pacific of Queen Charlotte Sound. They may hold the North American continent's all-time record for shipwrecks.

The overwhelmingly lonely trail from Holberg to Cape Scott is dotted with abandoned homesteads, mute testimony to the horrendous efforts of early pioneers to wrest a livelihood from this harsh land. The poignant Ronning farm in San Josef Valley, long abandoned, still is surrounded by tree species from around the world. A Canadian Armed Forces Air Base near Holberg was continued after World War II as a permanent radar establishment, really quite nicely set up with hospital, school and recreational facilities made available to visitors and local residents. The northern island is full of surprises. Hikers spend a deal of their time wringing the rain out of their sleeping bags but they come out starry-eyed with the wonder of it all.

When Island Highway is completed through to Port Hardy, and this community becomes southern port for the Queen of Prince Rupert and its flood of tourists, the northern island of

The traffic through Johnstone Strait, ranging from luxury liners
on Alaska runs to sturdy little gillnetters, adds much
to the pleasure of the trip on the ferry Island Princess.
Here a small sloop has raised her luff sail to trap the winds
coursing down this magnificent channel between Vancouver
Island, mainland islands and the coast of British Columbia.

coastal rain forest and solitude will change, its roads and facilities improve. Certainly it will be easier to visit, but integration with the remainder of Vancouver Island inevitably will rob its people of some of their distinctive pioneer spirit. If you can take its hardships — and they're not to be treated lightly, demanding planning and preparation — now is an interesting time to explore this virgin country far removed from the usual tourist experience. If you don't carry a real head of steam for adventure, don't try it.

Even if you find a trickly map line indicating steamer route up the west coast of Vancouver Island, this freight-passenger run to miniscule west coast communities was discontinued when it became possible to reach them via "industrial", i.e. restricted roads and the sea freight routes out of Port Alberni and Gold River. The old freight boats took up to 200 passengers, each absolutely thrilled out of his wits by sailing the horrendous "graveyard of the Pacific". The seven-day round trips were maintained by the Canadian Pacific's Princess Maquinna and the relief ship Princess Norah out of Victoria for Port Alice for forty years.

Occasionally the great seas sweeping off Cape Cook, most desolate and isolated coast of British Columbia, totally uninhabited, turned them back, extending the voyages. Their schedules were highly flexible, compounded of fog, weather, tide, and people emergencies. Not even vestiges of roads had been constructed, and the ubiquitous seaplane had not yet emerged. The Princess Maquinna was the life line of the west coast.

People who sailed on her assure me that the trip was scenically on a par with an Alaska cruise, and in some ways even more fun. The steamer stopped at every Indian village, cannery, fish reduction plant and floating logging camp, and spent a good day at Port Alice loading pulp for the south-bound run. Ah progress! It ends many joys. If it kills you to know that the

Johnstone Strait traffic includes many lumber barges under tow by sturdy little tugs, coming from remote logging camps of North Island to the mills of the southern towns.

west coast cruises are history now, it will be a comfort to learn about Northland Navigation (Passenger Department, 404 Hornby Street, Vancouver), which runs a similar service, freight, mail and passengers, weekly up the British Columbia mainland coast to Bella Coola, Ocean Falls, Kitimat, Prince Rupert, Port Simpson, Kincolith and Alice Arm, sometimes stopping off at Alert Bay on the southbound run.

Better still, Northland Navigation services the Haida Indians' Queen Charlotte Islands way out in Hecate Strait, just this side of the Alaska line. One ship sails Vancouver to Masset on North Graham Island with ports of call at Butedale and Prince Rupert. Another sails weekly for Queen Charlotte City at the southern end of Graham Island with ports of call at Alert Bay, Port McNeill, Port Hardy, Namu, Bella Bella and Klemtu. Even if they weren't so comfortable, the Northland Prince and Skeena Prince are first-rate adventure. Canadians reserve staterooms on them months of even years ahead, demand is so great.

Two of the finest of all boat trips available to visitors to Vancouver Island are provided by the Uchuck 111, which carries freight, mail and passengers throughout the tremendous arms and inlets of Nootka Sound on the West Coast. Here at dawn the Uchuck puts in at Tahsis, at the headwaters of Tahsis Inlet, on her two-day journey to Zeballos. Her second voyage available to visitors, concluded in one day, visits the Nootka Indian village Yuquot, at the mouth of Nootka Sound, the cove called "Friendly" by Captain James Cook, first white man to land on the west coast of Canada.

20 THE WEST COAST'S NOOTKA SOUND

This is where it all began.

Nootka Sound is a time tunnel to British Columbia's birth, site of an historical baring of teeth between the Spanish and British that came within an eyelash of setting off an international war. An excellent paved sixty-five-mile highway from Campbell River reaches the headwaters of Muchalat Inlet, twenty-five-mile-long arm of the fjord, near the instant town Gold River. Any history buff, and particularly those enthralled with the accomplishments of that magnificent navigator, Captain James Cook, R.N., will delight in knowing that he can reach the very spot on which Cook set foot at the Indian whaling settlement called Yuquot, "village exposed to the winds", at the mouth of Nootka Sound. He was the first European captain who dared to make a landing, a catalyst who set off an unbelievable era of international exploration which finally brought the Russians down the Aleutian chain to "Russian America" — Alaska.

Captain Cook was abetted in the advancement of exploration of the north coast decades ahead of the due course of events by a beguiling creature called the sea otter, coveted for its rich, glossy pelt. The value of sea otter fur in far eastern trade was cause celebre of the turmoil which almost tossed half the civilized world into conflict.

On a Sunday morning in March, 1778, the great English mariner, on his third voyage to the world's far places, set foot on island soil. The first visitor to this corner of earth may have been Greek navigator Juan de Fuca who in 1592, in the service of Spain, claimed to have discovered the strait that bears his name.

99

One of the treasures of Friendly Cove is this stained glass
church window, long-ago gift of Spain to the Indians in memory
of Franciscan missionary Padre Magin Catala
who served here during the Spanish occupation of the cove.
The window shows Hesquiat Indians of the Nootka tribe
in their customary garments, kootsiks (capes) and conical hats
woven from the inner bark of cedar. Padre Catala served
the west coast Indians of Vancouver Island from 1794 to 1830,
the first Christian cleric on the island. The window is located
at Saint Pius X Church, near the landing of the Uchuck 111.

There may have been more fiction than fact in his account, as he misplaced the strait on sea charts, but there is nothing imaginary about the exploration in 1774 of the Spaniard Juan Josef Perez Hernandez, and a year later of his compatriot Juan Francisco de la Bodega y Quadra. Both charted the west coast of Vancouver Island but feared to make landings in rough seas at inlets to thickly forested hills among an unknown and possibly hostile people.

Thus it was Cook's HMS Resolution and HMS Discovery that first rounded the rocks at Yuquot Point and dropped anchor at Resolution Cove on Bligh Island. Their commander was governed by practical needs. His water casks were near empty, and he had spotted giant cedar trees on the island that later was named for Vice-Admiral William Bligh — "Breadfruit" Bligh of the Bounty — who was navigating officer of the Resolution. These great trees would make straight new spars to replace those of the Resolution, smashed in offshore storms.

While the month-long work of repair progressed at Resolution Cove, the British seamen began a barter with the magnificent Maquinna, Chief of the Hesquiats, and Wickaninnish of the Clayoquots south of Nootka Sound, in the twenty longhouses of the village-exposed-to-the-winds.

Now the Hesquiat Indians were known the length of the coast as the greatest of whale hunters, setting out in seven-man canoes in pursuit of whales far off that violent shore. Frequently they came across pods of sea otters, and took them for their beautiful fur — valued for trade with inland tribes. Coastal Indians wore kootsiks (capes) and conical hats woven from the inner bark of cedar, using sea otter pelts in warm outer garments for winter wear and as bedding.

Casually it all began, the British giving the Indians bits of iron, sheets of copper and trinkets in exchange for the furs. True value of the glossy, inch-long fur of fine, close-packed fibers

A small seaplane service operates out of the headwaters of Muchalat Inlet to all points of the vast arms of Nootka Sound. Flights over the wild West Coast country are wonderful, affording views of hundreds of islands, snow-capped mountain peaks, great forests and valleys. Here a plane takes off from Tahsis, at the headwaters of Tahsis Inlet.

was not realized until Chinese merchants in Macao bid fortunes for these skins, up to $3000 for a single six-foot fur. Captain Cook's journals set off a gold rush, expeditions fitting out at London, Boston and Calcutta to exploit this bonanza. Hundreds of thousands of sea otter pelts eventually graced the luxury loving courts of Imperial Russia and the Chinese Dragon Empire. Siberian Promyshleniki were lured across the Bering Sea into the Aleutian chain, where they made otter-hunting slaves of the Aleuts.

Nootka Sound became the most important Pacific port north of San Francisco, as many as thirty ships of "King George's men", Russia, Spain and the "Boston men" crowding the cove Captain Cook called "Friendly" in honor of his amicable relationship with Chief Maquinna. Navigators considered that Nootka Sound, penetrating in three deep fjords far into the snow-capped mountains of the island's interior, was destined to become the great port of the Pacific shores of the Americas.

Here British Captain John Meares built the North West America, first ship constructed on the coast, and stood by helplessly when the Spaniards took possession of his ships and other English craft and sailed them with prize crews to San Blas, Mexico. The scene was set for the Nootka Controversy, which brought Europe to the brink of war before Spain backed down from her claim to the North Pacific, the first contraction of the mighty Spanish Empire.

This was not the end of skullduggery over the sea otter. Murder, treason, piracy—almost no form of violence was unknown as the fever increased. Chief Maquinna, grown arrogant from fawning attentions of rival captains, captured the American ship Boston in 1803 and burned her to the waterline. Twenty-five of her officers and men were murdered in return for some fancied slight to Maquinna's dignity by the Boston's Captain John Salter.

Trading continued at fierce pace until the latter part of the nineteenth century when at last the gentle little sea mammal was declared virtually extinct. In 1911 international laws were passed to protect the few remaining sea otters, most of them around Amchitka Island in the Aleutians with a small pod in kelp beds off Monterey Bay in California. The first evidence of their return in numbers in the thousands was observation of American soldiers, stationed at Amchitka during World War II, who wrote home about "goofy little animals" cavorting in the white caps and displaying the playful gayety that makes all land and sea otters so engaging. Most endearing is the female's trait of nursing her offspring cuddled in her arms as she floats on her back in the cradle of the waves.

I long knew that nothing much remains in the silent wilderness of the west coast of this page in world history but a ghost village at Yuquot, used by the Indians mostly as a summer fishing camp; a stained glass church window, long-ago gift of Spain in memory of Franciscan missionary Padre Magin Catala who served at Nootka during the Spanish occupation; and a lighthouse on rocks which were claimed by Spain as Fort San Miguel. Everyone who has ventured beyond the end of the road will have known my feeling. I just had to stand on the rocks where Captain James Cook planted the flag of British Empire.

21 CRUISING ON THE UCHUCK III

Serving the far flung ports of Nootka Sound.

At the head of Muchalat Inlet at last, I caught the coastal passenger-freighter M.V. Uchuck III through Muchalat Inlet and around Bligh Island to Cook's "Friendly Cove". The Uchuck, a sturdy 136-foot workhorse of a ship, serves all the far-flung ports of Nootka Sound, sailing six days a week year-round, "stopping at any raised broomstick". Her one-day trip to Friendly Cove is a tourist cruise, departing on Mondays and Wednesdays from late June to the end of August, a fifty-three mile sea voyage of incredible beauty. There's a layover at Friendly Cove, allowing time for a look at tottering totem poles, the mission church and the site of construction of the North West America.

My objective always is a scramble over sea-washed rocks to a lonely cairn of uncut stone, which can be reached on foot only when the tide is low. It was erected by the Historical Sites and Monuments Board of Canada to record Cook's landing. The simple cairn has a powerful effect upon viewers. I weep by it for the awful end to Cook's career a year later in the "Sandwich Isles", a cruel death at fifty-one years of age with a Polynesian spear in his back.

Looking out upon the untouched savage beauty of the west coast, you realize fully the courage and competence of eighteenth century sea captains who dared to enter the unknown, searching for the fabled Northwest Passage to the riches of India and filling in Earth's blank spaces. I wondered how Cook's seamen had felt, stepping ashore among 1500 barbaric, painted people armed with whaling harpoons. James Cook as easily

This touching simple, lonely cairn of uncut stone can be reached at Yuquot Point, near Friendly Cove, only when the tide is low enough for a scramble over sea-washed rocks. A memorial to Captain James Cook, first white man to set foot upon the Pacific Coast of Canada, it was erected by the Historical Sites and Monuments Board of Canada at the spot where Cook put ashore from his ships Resolution and Discovery.

could have lost his life here. No wonder he named Maquinna's village "Friendly", for acceptance of himself and his men must have brought with it an overpowering surge of relief.

According to a spokesman for the village, fisherman Jerry Jack, local skippers will charter their small craft for exploration and fishing, but anyone who remains between the Uchuck's visits must take along sleeping bag, camping gear and food.

Estevan Point, at the southern tip of the sound, is site of an important lighthouse. It is the only place in Canada shelled in World War II. A Japanese submarine surfaced two miles off shore and plastered the beach for forty minutes, fragments hitting a few buildings.

A small charter service flying out of Muchalat dock will take you over this wondrous country to Tahsis, where you can catch the Uchuck on her return trip from Esperanza Inlet to the mining and logging camp at Zeballos. Or you can fly from Vancouver Airport on regularly scheduled six-days-per-week flights to Tahsis at the head of Tahsis Inlet with Pacific Western Airlines or with British Columbia Airlines. Check schedules. They change seasonally. No difficulty with accommodations here, as one of the Delta Hotels' luxurious wilderness chalets, Tahsis Inn, is located near the seaplane wharf.

Flight in a small amphibious plane in clear weather over the Nootka complex has few equals for scenic glory anywhere in the world. Muchalat and Tlupana Arms, Tahsis and Esperanza Inlets, are backed up by glaciered peaks. Most spectacular of all is a thin cone-shaped peak I'd never heard of before, Conuma Peak, used by navigators and airmen as a landmark at the head of Tlupana Arm. As your plane is likely to set down at remote logging camps and mine docks en route, a passenger has that rare opportunity to view uninhabited islands, forests and lakes of a largely virgin country.

Pacific Western Airlines' winter morning flight from Vancouver Airport to north coast points in the pale citron and rose sky of first dawn is an experience so lyrically lovely that I repeat it on the flimsiest of excuses. Below is a mystique world, a vast island expanse puddled in darkness with here and there a lonely light of man, tugs and fish boats like a child's bathtub toys wrinkling the inland sea with long pale streamers of wake. Suddenly a weak winter sun tips over the Coast Range, setting aglitter immense glaciers and ice walls. A long finger of light silhouettes a loaded log carrier against a glow of gold across Queen Charlotte Strait, revealing a tidal rip circling in whirlpool vortex. I'm in seventh heaven.

It is because of recent developments in forest products industries in the Nootka area that there exists a land link and facilities with such promise for visitors. The Danish-owned East Asiatic Company, owner of Tahsis mills, one of the world's greatest sawmills, constructed a bleached kraft pulp mill at the head of Muchalat Inlet. To house its people, the model instant town Gold River came into being, inland about nine miles from the pulp mill. Logging began on the west coast in a limited way as early as 1914. In recent years, hundreds of ships a year sail into Nootka Sound to take the mill's lumber to world markets, and more ships head up Muchalat Inlet to load pulp.

This quiet new development is a boon to sportsmen, who now can reach fishing and hunting country almost unknown on the outside. The area still is sparsely settled. Gold River, its metropolis, boasts 3500 population; Tahsis mill workers and families number 1300. Prior to 1940, two trappers and one prospector were Tahsis Inlet's total inhabitants.

The inlets all are fed by fast, clean spawning rivers descending from Strathcona Park. Winter and summer steelhead runs in Gold River, Tahsis and Russian Rivers, Conuma and Tlupana Rivers offer superb sport. Seaplanes can be chartered to remote trout lakes in the interior. Fishing for chinooks and cohos is

108

great in the salt inlets. There's a boat launching ramp at the end of the cross-island road, Highway No. 28. Deer, elk, bear and cougar interest hunters. Trails follow ancient Indian routes barely indicated on maps. The peaks of the region for the most part never have been climbed.

In due time I caught the Uchuck back from Tahsis. The customers and their accoutrements are as interesting as the route and may include absolutely everything from a black bear hide to an inflatable boat. As we neared Tahsis Narrows, Captain Esson Young, the most amiable of men with a bottomless store of tales of his untamed land and its history and a lovely habit of sharing his wheelhouse coffee pot with interested listeners, tole me to climb to the roof of the wheelhouse. Once up I knew why. There before my dazzled eyes was one of the most wildly beautiful views in all British Columbia. The Rugged Mountains rose straight up from the headwaters of the inlet in wave upon wave of thick forest to lofty heights of shattered, crenelated rock.

As I looked up the long sweep of the blue, blue Narrows, suddenly two dimples appeared on the glass-smooth surface of the water and two sleek, bright-eyed, curious heads broke water and peered at our passage, rolling up to float on their backs in our wake. I held my breath, hardly daring to hope that I was seeing a pair of sea otters. Back in the wheelhouse, Captain Young asked me,

"You see the otters following us?"

If this journey into history offered nothing more, I would have been content with that wondrous moment.

22 INSTANT TOWN—GOLD RIVER

The final outpost to the northern interior.

At Gold River is located another of the Delta Hotels' snug havens, a beauty of a chalet with every comfort including a heated outdoor pool and resident fishing guide, a fine "fixer" for guided trips. The town of Gold River, incorporated as a district municipality in August of 1965 under the "instant town" legislation passed in the same year, is as improbable in the fastness of the west coast as the chalet—all new and beautifully planned for the good life for its pulp mill people.

Gold River is the final outpost before entering the near-untrodden world of the island's northern interior, a vast unpopulated land little changed in the 130-year modern history of Vancouver Island. Gold River is the start of a 100-mile logging road to Beaver Cove on the northeast coast through the Nimpkish Valley, most of it along an ancient Indian route. This road system, formed by linking up a maze of private logging roads, provides the only overland route to North Island. It is called the Canfor Road, for Canadian Forest Products, Ltd, holders of Nimpkish Tree Farm Licence No. 37 which covers almost the entire valley. Canfor's private timber and lands have been combined here with Crown forests which are being managed jointly for the permanent production of forest crops.

At one time the route was traveled by Vancouver Island Coach Lines which now drive north only to Vernon, Woss and Nimpkish on the shore of Nimpkish Lake, out of Campbell River on Sundays and Thursdays.

In recent times this restricted logging road, never easy to travel, has deteriorated in the span along Bonanza Lake until

110

coach drivers advise, "It's worth your life to try it". Frankly, I'm scared of it. Canfor makes its roads available to the public only if at the same time it can carry on efficient logging operations. This makes the tourist low man on the totem pole.

If I harp at length on restricted roads, there's a reason for my fear. I've driven over hundreds of miles of British Columbia's restricted roads without any special incident, but there's something stuck in memory. Years ago, long before the route up the Fraser Canyon became a part of the Trans-Canada Highway and was re-engineered at the cost of around a million dollars per mile to its current excellence, I started up it in the days of trembling wooden trestles hung over its abyss. I was just a kid, newly licenced to drive.

At a particularly hairy one-lane span of switchbacks up a canyon wall, I met a logging truck, a monstrous logging truck. The rules require that the passenger car back down for trucks, not vice versa, despite the general dewiness of this nouveau driver. I had to back down the Fraser Canyon a half-mile over tortuous road horrendous to face going forward! Finally I found a narrow ledge where I could turn off, and let the behemoth by. It left a lasting impression. When I quit shaking I chickened out and turned back. Subliminal fear of logging trucks still is very much with me. I respect their priority and also the terrible weight of the balanced loads pushing their cabs at high speed.

Travel on the Canfor is permitted on weekends and holidays and between the hours of five in the afternoon and six in the morning, Mondays through Fridays. Restrictions are subject to change and closure at any time due to weather, fire, hazards or increased logging operations. There is no warranty on condition of the roads, which at the very best are suffocatingly dusty in summer, requiring lights on at all hours. Permits are issued by gatemen at either end.

Camping is restricted to company-designated areas at Woss

111

Lake, Vernon Lake, Schoen Lake and near the mouth of the Nimpkish River. Camps are closed in periods of high fire hazard. Services in the Nimpkish Valley are for the convenience and use of the small logging communities which overall have a total population of fewer than 1000 men, women and children. However coffee bars, gas and service stations, company commissaries and First Aid rooms may be used by visitors. Bunkhouse and cookhouse are for employees only. There is no housing, and food supplies for camping should be carried in from Gold River or Port McNeill.

With all this, the wild Nimpkish Valley holds enormous lure for hunters and fishermen who want to try new areas, and try them they do, generally with four-wheel-drive vehicles. There's an information center located at Woss which will provide dope on state of the road. I vastly prefer the opinion of the professional drivers, and am willing to let them do the driving for me, luv.

23 STRATHCONA

A wilderness sanctuary in the center of the island.

Half way between Campbell River and Gold River, at almost the exact center of Vancouver Island, is Strathcona Provincial Park, a vast mountainous wilderness of more than a half million acres. Bless Canada for designating it a wildlife sanctuary in which vehicles (trail motorcycles, snowmobiles, ATVs, etc.) are not allowed and firearms sternly are prohibited. Herds of elk range its fastnesses. Deer, black bear, wolverine, cougar and even wolves live within its ancient red cedar, Douglas fir, balsam and hemlock forests. Wildflowers flourish on sub-alpine meadows in spectacular display through the summer months, great beds of heather, lupine, monkey flower, violets, Indian paintbrush, alpine phlox and moss campion gentling the spans between innumerable mountain lakes and streams.

The major body of water, Buttle Lake, and many other lakes and waterways provide good fishing for cutthroat trout, rainbows and Dolly Vardens. Three totally roadless tracts within Strathcona — Big Den, Central Strathcona and Comox Glacier with a total area in excess of 300,000 acres — are set aside as nature conservancies, dedicated to preservation of the natural environment. Just two regions, Buttle Lake and Forbidden Plateau, have some visitor developments. To enjoy its greatest scenic splendour you must backpack in and up.

Only recent maps carry indication of the splendid new paved road extending south from cross-island Highway No. 28 the full length of Buttle Lake and around its southern tip to Myra Falls. Distance is about twenty-five or thirty miles. The road was constructed along the lake shore as access to Western Mines, high grade copper producer on Myra Creek, and to open the park to vacationists. There are well-marked boat launching areas and one of the finest campgrounds, Ralph River, on the island. Another very good camping area is Buttle Lake Campgrounds, just off Highway No. 28 west of the bridge over the connecting channel between Upper Campbell and Buttle Lakes. Elk Falls, outside Strathcona Park five miles west of Campbell River, is a third convenient campsite. Thus at long last the wilderness park, the wonder of the central heart of the island, is available to more than the cleated boot and packboard crowd.

There are cautions. Only experienced mountaineers properly roped and equipped with ice axes should attempt the 7000-foot climbs. Some trails are in good shape, and more are being added annually. Others such as the overgrown route from the head of Great Central Lake to Della Falls should be attempted only with an experienced guide able to use a compass and read a contour map. A trail of sorts follows Drinkwater Creek for ten or twelve miles, crossing frequently without benefit of bridges. It can be impassable in high water periods.

Even reaching the Della Falls trailhead is a problem, requiring arrangement with a water taxi to travel the length of Great Central Lake from end of the road at the east end of the lake to the start of the trail near the western end. Those who have seen the falls flip. You may never have heard of Della Falls, peculiarly neglected in rosters of the world's great cascades. The highest in Canada, ninth highest in the world, it drops 1,443 feet in three majestic falls.

Day hikes into Strathcona from Forbidden Plateau are over well-marked trail to Mount Becher, Douglas and Mackenzie Lakes and the base of Mount Colonel Foster. Longer hikes include summit ascents over snowfields of Mount Albert

114

Edward, the Golden Hinde, highest point on Vancouver Island at 7219 feet, and Elkhorn Mountain.

For more information on Strathcona, write Parks Branch, Department of Recreation and Conservation, Parliament Buildings, Victoria. Large-scale detailed maps are available at modest fee from Director, Surveys and Mapping Branch, Geographic Division; Department of Lands, Forests and Water Resources, Parliament Buildings, Victoria.

There is no lodge within Strathcona outside of a skiers' day lodge at Forbidden Plateau, but near the park boundary, on Upper Campbell Lake, is a rustic log-constructed old timer overlooking a span of the lakes, surrounded by great peaks. Strathcona Park Lodge is managed by teachers Jim and Myrna Boulding, graduates of Reading University of England, specialists in the arts of Pacific rain forest survival and all facets of woodsmanship. Jim has been a Class A guide for twelve years.

In keeping with their prime interest — teaching survival techniques to the young and to the teachers of the young — the Bouldings each year host seven coeducational outdoor summer camps for young men and women ages thirteen to eighteen. Cottages adjacent to the Lodge are home port, with overnight outings by canoe and by trail to studies in ecology and survival, boat handling and safety, outdoor first aid, camping, climbing, fishing and general woodsmanship. The University of British Columbia, Vancouver, B.C., through its Centre for Continuing Education sponsors the annual course for university students. Boulding's staff, who know the trails of Strathcona like the backs of their hands, serves as guides to climbing parties. The address is Strathcona Lodge, Box 216, Campbell River.

*The West Coast's fabulous Long Beach,
extending for 12 uninterrupted miles along
Wickaninnish Bay, often is piled with masses of
driftwood logs heaped as casually as matchsticks.
One great storm brings them in, and the next
well may sweep them all away. So mercilessly are
the beaches of Esowista Peninsula pounded
by the winter swells that there is a seasonal
difference of six feet in the sand level.*

24 THE WEST COAST

Voyages with the Lady Rose.

The second great highway that crosses the island is a cinch, wide, paved Highway No. 4 extending twenty-nine miles from Parksville to Port Alberni at the headwaters of Alberni Inlet. Amazingly, this arm of Barkley Sound reaches within twelve crowflight miles of the east coast of Vancouver Island and thus is the longest of all the fjords of the west coast. Alberni Highway is a beauty, running along the shore of fish-rich Cameron Lake, a jewel in the central mountains (pleasant picnic site here and boat launching ramp, with nearby trailhead of hikers' route up awesome 5962-foot Mount Arrowsmith). The second treat is Cathedral Grove of MacMillan nature park, a virgin forest preserve set aside for public enjoyment during logging of the general area. The grove's great Douglas firs and cedars grow so closely-knit that it is forever twilight on its nature trails, and no more than misty below even in heavy rain.

*The twenty-six-mile coastline from Ucluelet to
Tofino, most of which is incorporated in new
Pacific Rim National Park, has innumerable
gentle little coves such as this one, near
Wickaninnish Inn. They're great for
beachcombing treasure ranging from semi-precious
stones to remnants of historic wrecks,
uncovered in storms.*

25 PORT ALBERNI

Steelhead and sawmills.

Port Alberni, a handsome town of wide residential streets, grew up around huge sawmills, a pulp and paper mill, but by no means does it neglect its fishing rivers and lakes and its superb boating down that long finger of the sea. Two boat ramps and a busy marina are located in the heart of town and nearby Sproat Lake is dotted with resorts and boat landings. Stamp Falls Provincial Campgrounds is located nine miles north of Port Alberni on the Beaver Creek Road—a fascinating spot for children to watch homecoming salmon leaping and wriggling up a large fish ladder in the fall. Sproat Lake, eight miles west of Port Alberni on Sproat Lake Road, has a fair-sized (forty unit) camping area with a swimmers' change-house for day visitors.

Steelhead fishing is possible year-round with the best months February, June, August and September. Stamp, Somass, Franklin and Nahmint Rivers, China Creek and the famous "Money's Pool" on the Ash River boast steelie runs that bring fishermen from all over the island. The big chinooks to sixty pounds are taken in Alberni Inlet, heading for their home rivers, in August and September. With all this, Port Alberni, the major gateway to the Pacific, has an abundance of fresh, new motels, among them Tyee Village, the Green Door, Redford Motor Inn and Timber Lodge.

Winter's wild storms on the West Coast mean
treasure for beachcombers who find on these
beaches Japanese and Russian fishnet floats as big
as basketballs, in colors ranging from pale
sea green to deep purple. Bamboo poles shoved
by currents across the Pacific, wine casks, whale
vertebrae, hatch covers and beautiful shells all
are found by strollers.

26 THE LADY ROSE

Queen of Barkley Sound.

The prime tourist attraction is a doughty little ship called the MV Lady Rose which for years has carried mail, cargo and happy passengers through one hundred miles of wilderness to small fishing communities at the mouth of Barkley Sound — Ucluelet and Bamfield, with way stops at logging camps, canneries and fishermen's havens. Built in Scotland in 1937, the Lady Rose came out to British Columbia under her own power, testimony to her seaworthiness.

Her captain is a remarkable man, John Monrufet, handsome, affable veteran of sailing Canada's Arctic Coast, the Mackenzie River of Northwest Territories and the west coast of Vancouver Island. In the past twelve years, the Lady Rose has missed sailing from the foot of Argyle Street at eight in the morning on just one day of hurricane force winds. Fog so thick you can serve it as soup doesn't faze her. Confided one of her regulars to me,

"If John has a six-inch clearance he'll make it. On many a winter day he navigates by the echo of the ship's horn through those narrow passages, running a blind slalom course through hundreds of small islands and rocks at the mouth of the sound." He routes his ship directly under the bow of the Vanlene, hung on the rocks of the Deer Islands, for a thrilling close-up look at the most recent of the wrecks that dot Barkley Sound. Remember the Vanlene? In storm and fog her captain believed she was somewhere off the Oregon Coast. Her cargo of Japanese automobiles is still in the hold, impossible to salvage.

The Lady Rose is an unpretentious work boat, but she can carry up to 100 passengers. For days of bad weather there's a

The West Coast's fabulous Long Beach, extending for 12 uninterrupted miles along Wickaninnish Bay is at the heart of Phase 1 of development of Canada's first national park on the Pacific, Pacific Rim National Park.

lounge, and the coffee shop operates continuously. Her current schedule calls for sailings on Mondays, Wednesdays and Fridays for Ucluelet, on Tuesdays and Thursdays for Bamfield through channels called Imperial Eagle, Loudon and Trevor. On the long trip — Ucluelet — she's back at her home port at around six-thirty in the evening. On Bamfield sailings, return is at four in the afternoon, give or take a bit for flag stops.

Barkley Sound, a fabulously beautiful fifteen-mile-wide body of water is named for its discoverer, British Captain Charles William Barkley; Imperial Eagle Channel for his full-rigged ship of 400 tons, Trevor Channel after the maiden name of his young wife.

This brave little girl deserves more mention than that. She married Captain Barkley after a whirlwind courtship in the Protestant Chapel, Ostend, Belgium, in 1786 at the age of just seventeen years, and immediately thereafter departed with her husband on a series of voyages to Nootka Sound. There Captain Barkley bartered with the Indians for sea otter and other furs, crossing the Pacific to China where he disposed of his cargo at considerable gain to the ship. His bride was the first white woman the Nootkas ever had seen. A tidy little body much given to starched petticoats and good housewifery in the captain's quarters, the little girl mistress of the Imperial Eagle was considerably shook up at the work-horse lot of life of Indian women, among the world's worst victims of male pig chauvinism.

On the Barkleys' first visit to Yuquot, they rescued a disillusioned Dr. John Mackay, a surgeon's mate who had been left at Friendly Cove a year before at his own request. The magnanimous doctor hoped to serve the Indians, and he wanted to test the agricultural potential of Nootka should a white settlement be established there. He was friendly enough with Chief Maquinna, planting rows of vegetables under the skeptical eyes of the Indians. When his crops matured, he attempted to enlarge the Indian diet, but under no circumstances could they be induced to eat this strange fodder. Emaciated, despondent, and now treated with considerable scorn by his hosts, Dr. Mackay took off like a shot at first sight of the Imperial Eagle. Prissy little missy Barkley was horrified.

"His dress and appearance, the same as the native, was, to say the least, disgusting. The surprise when he introduced himself as Dr. John Mackay to Captain Barkley and myself was great indeed."

The voyages of the Lady Rose are the easiest and most pleasant ways to reach two storied areas of intense beauty. A restrictèd logging road about sixty-plus miles in length does extend from Port Alberni through mountains and logged-over land to Bamfield, but I have yet to hear a single good word for it. Long ago, hikers of the West Coast Trail, the old Life Saving Trail which follows the Pacific Coast for forty-five miles between Bamfield and Port San Juan near Renfrew, learned to reach Bamfield with their gear on the Lady Rose or by float plane — not overland.

Bamfield once was an important station for the trans-Pacific cable between Canada and New Zealand-Australia, but cable operations have been moved to Port Alberni. The old station now is used by universities for biological research. The town is a fishing hamlet, site of a small outpost hospital, but it does have one of two life-saving stations maintained on the west coast. There's a small lodge, Aguilar House, a sort of hikers' headquarters open from May through December, and a few cabins at nearby Brady's Beach with boat rentals and moorage.

27 THE LIFE SAVING TRAIL

Wilderness challenge for the young in spirit.

Total population about 250, Bamfield is basking in new glory now that adventure-bound American backpackers have discovered the Life Saving Trail in phenomenal numbers. First hacked out of the thick brush along the coast in 1890, the famous trail saved the lives of many seamen stranded by wrecked vessels off that wicked coast which in the past 100 years has taken a toll of one shipwreck per mile. A telephone line was strung from tree to tree, eventually all the way to Port Renfrew, and cabins containing emergency food, clothing and first aid supplies erected every few miles. The trail was patrolled and maintained, its crew fairly often finding shipwrecked men too weak to attempt travel without help.

Eventually modern navigation aids and two great lighthouses at Pachena and Carmanah reduced the usefulness of the trail. Unfortunately it was abandoned to the wilds in 1954. Soon the forest crept back in, salal swallowing miles of the route. Blowdown fell across the trail, wiping out every trace; ladders rotted and gave way, and suspension foot bridges over rivers collapsed.

Now the trail is included as Phase Three of Canada's first great park on the sea, Pacific Rim National Park, centered on the Esowista Peninsula between Ucluelet and Tofino. Phase Two is the Effingham Islands, beauteous humps at the mouth of Barkley Sound. In the last few years the Parks Department has sent teams of university students over the trail in summers to attempt its re-opening. It now has become "passable", a euphemism requiring a long stretch of the imagination.

Detailed maps may be obtained from the Map Production

*Alert Bay, Cormorant Island, an Indian fishing
and logging village near the northern tip of
Vancouver Island, is famed for its magnificent
totems and Kwakiutl Indian artifacts.*

Division, Department of Lands, Forests and Water Resources in Victoria; current trail information from check-in points at either end of the trail. You have to register in and out, and you'll be turned down flat if you are not adequately equipped to face a strenuous week's outing. It's costly and hazardous to lift out by helicopter those who conk out en route. Tide tables are vital to safety.

The first span, about two hours easy walking to Pachena Point Lighthouse, is pure joy. Many will want to stop right here, way before the going gets tough. Ahead is a battle with head-high tangles of salal, tremendous beauty of rock-bound coast and hidden coves jammed with sea-battered driftwood, lush forest and ragged reefs straggling out to sea, a modicum of danger of being caught by the incoming tide while rounding great headlands thrust out into the sea, rivers that must be waded with camping gear held over the head, ominous caves furred with seaweed, clefts in the rock booming with incoming waves at high tide, a discouraging series of ladders with missing rungs, trembling bridges, wet and slippery fallen-log stream crossings, quagmires of mud, windfall piled like matchsticks, slippery notched logs inviting sprained ankles, and other little pleasures. The last dozen miles combine the whole works and may require two full days to traverse, especially as it's almost always raining in the area, which gets a good 200 inches annually.

If you make it to Port Renfrew, there's a wee problem of getting back to your car at Port Alberni. For once, there's no coach line service. You have to hitch hike into Victoria. Port Renfrew loggers are used to people emerging from the trail looking like Sasquatches. Your disheveled state won't scare them off. From Sooke or Victoria, travel is easy by public means to Port Alberni.

Is it worth it? Yes! But oh God, not alone. With all its delicious flavor of freedom, involving all the senses, it's overwhelming, a put down of man in a very inferior position to nature. You need fellow hikers with whom to laugh and quarrel over route and share your dehydrated applesauce. It reduced me — alone — to a quivering cup of jelly, a timid transgressor. The Life Saving Trail is one of the truly great wilderness challenges for the lithe of leg, the young in spirit. If half-drowned sailors traveled it to safety, it must once have been a tremendous trail. I'll be back when it is restored, probably when all the questions of boundary have been resolved.

On the 100 mile trip from Alberni to Ucluelet, the MV Lady Rose shows visitors a wonderful fjord which comes near to cutting Vancouver Island in two.

28 PACIFIC RIM NATIONAL PARK, THE GREAT BEACHES AND THAT AWESOME ROAD

Canada's first park on the Pacific.

The twenty-six mile expanse of Pacific beach between Ucluelet and Tofino on the west-central island coast, newly discovered by surfers, has few equals anywhere in the world. For sheer raw nature, only some of Australia's remote beaches can compare. The central twelve miles of quarter-mile-wide, clean, uninterrupted sands appears as Long Beach on most maps but still is called Wickaninnish Beach by the locals for the grand old chief who shared dominion over the west coast in the eithteenth century with the Hesquiats' Chief Maquinna.

Some 35,820 acres of which 22,000 acres are land and 13,820 acres are water form the initial development of Canada's first park on the Pacific. Pacific Rim National Park will incorporate three separate and different terrains identified as Phases One, Two and Three—Long Beach, the 100 or more Effingham Islands (Broken Island Group) at the mouth of Barkley Sound, and the Life Saving Trail. Phase One includes the area extending north-westerly from Wya Point, near Ucluelet Inlet, through Florencia (Wreck) Bay, Wickaninnish Bay, Schooner Cove, Portland Point, the Radar Beaches and Point Cox, turning easterly to include the foreshores of Grice and Indian Bays of Tofino Inlet. The inland boundary includes water frontage and back-up lands on Kennedy Lake, largest lake on Vancouver Island, to provide freshwater swimming and fishing. Altogether, it is a fabulous chunk of real estate with endless gifts for its visitors.

The second phase, that enchanting drift of islands of Barkley Sound, probably will remain in wilderness with little more

129

The West Coast's chief claim to fame is wrecks,
an incredible number of them, in the past
100 years one shipwreck per mile. Thus the coast
came into its sad title, "graveyard of ships."
With all modern navigational aids, ships still are
wrecked on shark's tooth reefs straggling out
to sea, tangles of rocky islands, and by the pull of
currents which drive them into headlands in
zero visibility weather. Seen from the deck of the
Lady Rose is the wreck of the Vanlene, which went
on the rocks of the Deer Islands in fog and storm.
Her cargo of Japanese automobiles
largely was lost.

development than marine parks on a few of the islands, fifty-two of which are large enough to warrant names.

The boundaries of the third phase, the Life Saving Trail, have not yet been determined. The trail commences at the estuary of the Gordon River at the head of Port San Juan, near Port Renfrew, and continues along the coast to include Owen Point, Carmanah Point, Pachena Point and Cape Beale (near Bamfield), a coastline distance of fifty-seven miles, trail distance forty-five miles. Proposals are being heard to enlarge the coastal strip far beyond protection of the historic trail, but there's a Catch Twenty-Two here. The combined coastline of Phases One and Three is about one hundred miles. Remarks the Honourable W. K. Kiernan, Minister of Recreation and Conservation,

"Would we be unwittingly creating problems for future development of the west coast hinterland behind the parks? In our desire to provide the utmost protection for the trail and its environment, might we not frustrate interior developments requiring access to the sea?"

The perfect way to reach Pacific Rim is via the Lady Rose to Ucluelet, where taxis and a few rental cars are available. Orient Stage Lines provide daily (except Saturdays) bus service over Highway No. 4 from May to October, departing Port Alberni at three in the afternoon for Ucluelet. Pacific Western Airlines maintains thrice-weekly scheduled flight from Vancouver to Tofino Airport, once an RCAF operational base. Ocean Air Limited flies seaplanes from Port Alberni twice daily to Tofino, which also has taxis and rental cars.

The Road
Highway No. 4 extends sixty-seven miles from Port Alberni to the park, with an added twenty-six mile span from Ucluelet to Tofino. This road, lifting up in switchbacks to the summit of

Looking directly down into one of Botany Bay's thousands of rock-and-sea sculpted tidal pools, the viewers sees exquisite creatures.

the Klitsa Mountains, has earned a regrettable reputation for tooth and tire-shattering chuckholes and heart-in-mouth mountain cliffhanging in a short span—now seventeen miles—which remains to be re-engineered and paved. About six miles of it, up and over the summit for tremendous views of Sproat Lake far below, is perfectly awful at customary highway speed. It isn't bad at all, even for me, if it is taken at a mild twenty miles an hour tops. By the summer of 1973, it is expected that the last bit of pavement will be rolled in place. It's a beautiful drive crossing rushing rivers sweet with the smell of wet forest growth, meandering along the shores of Kennedy Lake, frequently bound by canyon walls trickling with waterfalls and covered solidly with the most extravagant, incredible growth of maidenhair fern I've ever seen. I always have to leap out and photograph the ferns, just to convince myself that such a thing can be out of the tropics.

Pacific Rim National Park

Don't miss it, this coast of unsung splendor, at any time of the year. Long Beach is the best spot in the world to experience the ferocious grandeur of an autumn storm, mountainous seas trembling the earth, logs crashing and rumbling like trains in a subway tunnel as great Pacific combers send them surging in and out immediately beneath the enthralled viewer. There is a winter-summer variation as great as six feet in the sand level. One day winter's high tide line will be covered with huge tangles of driftwood and beached logs, the next swept clean by still another storm. An abandoned automobile, stuck in the sand, stands out like a sore thumb one afternoon and next morning can't be found.

This means treasure for beachcombers who find on these beaches Japanese and Russian glass fishnet floats as big as basketballs, pieces of wrecked ships that have come to grief

133

on this wild coast, bamboo poles shoved by currents across the Pacific, hatch covers and fish boxes, wicker-covered demijohns and wine casks, whale vertebrae, gorgeous shells and ship's lanterns. Heavy seas often expose historic wrecks and as quickly bury them again.

In summer the surf is mild enough — only a few degrees cooler than that of southern California beaches — for swimming and wading tidal pools in search of Dungeness crabs. There's good razor clam digging all along the sea-pounded beaches and fishing trips to be arranged with Indian captains of Tofino.

Troll up coast to the head of Hot Springs Cove near the entrance to Sydney Inlet. A mile and one-half trail through Maquinna Park then will take you to an enjoyable experience, a bath in rock pools under the ten-foot waterfalls of a steaming hot mineral spring. Facing the open Pacific, the pools can alternate in high spring tides from steaming hot sulphur water to a cold salt sea as waves sweep in and fill them momentarily, altogether a thrilling sensation. Local Indians believe in the curative powers of the water, especially for rheumatic ailments, bathing in it, drinking it, as do many west coast people.

On Flores Island, north boundary of Clayoquot Sound, Gibson Marine Park has been set aside in Matilda Inlet for boatsmen near the hot springs at Ahousat. A wild roadless island, Flores is a fascinating place to explore, its shores a series of open bays, via small boat out of Tofino.

By all means pick up at the park information center a copy of Pacific Rim's interpretive program which runs from late June through Labor Day weekend. For so new a park, there's a strong plan underway to assist visitors in understanding this lovely littoral, its giant forest trees and ocean shore teeming with marine life. There are self-guiding nature trails, conducted walks at Schooner Cove, Green Point, through the Rain Forest and an Ecology Hike, all short enough for children's participation.

Paths through the coastal forest lead to beaches of considerable variety. One is covered with egg-sized stones, polished and glistening. Another is studded with massive, kelp-covered boulders washed with mantillas of sea spray. A third beach offers pure white sand of finely crushed shells and warm protected swimming waters.

In the evenings there are color slide programs and, at Long Beach Campsite, a program which varies according to the interests of those who attend. Weekend boat tours are on tap summers to Sea Lion Rocks, just off Long Beach, allowing close-up view of large colonies of sea lions and nesting birds.

29 UCLUELET AND TOFINO

A scenic and fishing mecca with a growing artist's colony.

Set aside some time to explore Ucluelet and Tofino, each located on near-landlocked protected waters of tremendous beauty. Ucluelet is the third largest fishing port on Canada's west coast. Watch for signs on boat sheds offering such delicacies as seawater-boiled Dungeness crabs, fresh oysters and abalones, Indian-smoked salmon and steelhead, and the tiny, delectable shrimp of Barkley Sound, certainly worth the considerable effort to peel them.

Tofino rapidly is acquiring a resident artists' colony, with reason, and has opened a Maritime Museum. My special love, it is thrust out on a point of land in Clayoquot Sound. Just across its inlet is Opitisaht, chief village of the Clayoquot Indians, bound by lupine-covered sand dunes. An estimated 10,000 black brant winter on the tidal flats here, along with other species of ducks and geese, giving Tofino an enviable reputation for geese and duck shooting. The most glorious sunset I believe I've ever seen was from Opitisaht, looking across burnished flame-colored waters to a great red disk sinking into the sea. In the foreground were anchored fish boats and flights of seabirds, their wings catching the glitter as they lifted into that wondrous sky.

30 WHERE TO STAY

Varied enough to keep everyone happy.

You'll find no spartan discomfort at Pacific Rim. There's a large campground near the north end of Wickaninnish Bay with ninety secluded campsites separated by tall timbers. Its network of trails leads through carpets of thimbleberry, salal, wild strawberry and cascades of ferns to its own beautiful span of beach.

During World War II a first-class Canadian military airport operated near Tofino and an important radar installation was placed on the most spectacular of the coast promontories, long abandoned and now known to the natives as "Radar Hill". (There's a good road to its summit.) In the past two decades, sports pilots began to fly into the field for very special reasons. They loved the surfing beaches and the casual camping above the high tide line.

Flyers discovered Tofino's crab and salmon fleets and soon had going an annual fly-in, in July, highlighted by a beach seafood bake. No longer a fly-in, Tofino's two-day party now draws more people by automobile than by plane. Certainly it served as a stimulus to construction of the coast's few beach resorts.

The most luxurious resort up-island was Wickaninnish Inn, located on massive rocks thrust seaward at the southern end of the long stretch of beach. As the Inn is within park boundaries, its future is in limbo. Probably the building and surrounding 200 acres of private forest and beach will be incorporated into park facilities in some way—not as public lodge, however. A pleasant resort at Ucluelet is the West Coast Boatel. At Tofino,

Duffin Cove Cabins, reached by steep flight of log steps leading to the shore of Duffin Pass, looks right out upon the spectacular sunsets and the silhouetted fishing fleet hurrying home one hundred strong to protected waters of Clayoquot Sound.

Off Tofino, on little Stubbs Island out in Father Charles Channel, is an extraordinary place to stay — Clayoquot Lodge, a short boat ride from the town dock. The venerable lodge and widespread gardens were the private estate of a mining tycoon. Boats and guides are available here, and the lodge remains open year-round. As accommodations on Esowista Peninsula are in demand, reservations are advised, even in winter. Tofino's Chamber of Commerce will send a business directory with full listing.

INDEX

Active Pass, 27, 57, 58
Admiral of Coon Island, 54
Aguilar House, 124
Ahousat, 134
Airwest Airlines, 26
Alaska Ferries, 28
Alberni, 76
Alberni Highway, 117
Alberni Inlet, 21, 76, 117, 119
Alberni Marine
  Transportation Co., 32
Alert Bay, 32, 36, 86, 88, 92, 97
Alert Bay Air Services, 26
Alice Arm, 97
All Sooke Day, 52
Amchitka Island, 104
Anacortes, 26, 27
Antique Row, 42
April Point, 61, 64
April Point Fishing Resort, 63
April Point Yacht Club, 64
Ash River, 119

Bamfield, 22, 23, 32, 76, 121,
  123-125
Barbary Banjo, 40
Barkley, Captain Charles
  William, 123
Barkley Sound, 21, 32, 76, 117,
  121, 123, 129, 136
Bastion Square, 40, 42
Bastion (Nanaimo), 74, 75
Bathtub Regatta, 75
Beachcomber, The, 41
Beacon Hill, 35
Beaufort Sea, 11
Beaumont Marine Park, 57
Beaver Cove, 21, 23, 32, 86, 90,
  110
Beaver Creek Road, 119
Bedwell Harbour, 57
Bedwell Harbour Resort, 57
Beehive Wool, The, 45
Bella Bella, 97
Bella Coola, 97
Belleville Street, 35
Bellingall Islands, 58
Benvenuto, 47
Beresford Island, 93
Big Den, 113
Black Ball Transport, 26
Bligh Island, 101, 105
Bligh, Vice-Admiral
  William, 101
Blubber Bay, 32
Bonanza Lake, 111
Booth Bay Resort, 54, 57
Botanical Beach, 50
Botany Bay, 22, 50, 51

Boulding, Jim and Myrna, 115
Bowser, 76
Brady's Beach, 124
Brentwood Bay, 32, 49
British Columbia Airlines, 107
British Columbia Ferries, 25,
  28
B. C. Coast Ferries, 88
British Columbia Ferry
  Authority, 27
BC Forest Products, 65
British Columbia Tourist
  Directory, 25
Broken Island Group, 129
Broughton Strait, 90
Buckley Bay, 31, 59, 76
Butchart Gardens, 26, 32, 47
Butchart, Jennie, 14, 47, 48
Butchart, Robert Pim, 47, 48
Butedale, 97
Bute Inlet, 63
Butter Church, 67
Buttle Lake, 22, 113
Buttle Lake Campground, 114

Cameron Lake, 76, 117
Campbell River, 22, 31, 43, 61,
  62, 81, 82, 85, 99, 110, 113,
  114
Campbell River-Gold River
  Road, 22
Canadian Armed Forces
  Air Base, 93
Canadian Forest Products,
  Ltd., 110
Canadian Pacific, 26, 28, 95
Canfor Road, 110, 111
Cape Beale, 131
Cape Cook, 95
Cape Mudge, 62
Cape Mudge Lighthouse, 61,
  62, 75
Cape Scott, 93
Captain's Palace, The, 41
Carmanah, 125
Carmanah Point, 131
Cascade Range, 31
Catala, Padre Magin, 104
Cathedral Grove, 21, 117
Ceepeecee, 33
Centennial Building, 85
Centennial Square, 40
Central Strathcona, 113
Cheese and Wein Shop, 41
Chemainus, 31, 69
Cherry Bank Hotel, 41
Cheslakees Campsite, 90
Chez Ernest, 41
China Creek, 119

Chinese Village Restaurant, 41
Classic Car Museum, 42
Clayoquot Lodge, 138
Clayoquots, 101, 136
Clayoquot Sound, 134, 136,
  138
Clemclemaluts Catholic
  Mission Church, 67
Clo-oose, 75
Coach and Four, 40
Coal Harbour, 90
Coastal Ferry Service, 31
Coast Salish, 43
Comiaken, 67
Comox, 28, 78
Comox Glacier, 113
Comox Peak, 107
Conuma River, 108
Cook, Captain James, 33, 38,
  99, 103-105
Cormorant Island, 32, 86
Cortes Island, 20, 31, 62, 65
Cossack, The, 41
Courtenay, 24, 75, 78, 79
Cowichan Indians, 43, 45, 46,
  69, 70, 78
Cowichan Lake, 22
Cowichan River, 66
Cowichan River Valley, 67
Cowichan Trading Company,
  45, 46, 69
Cowichan Valley Forest
  Museum, 71, 73
Cox, 93
Craigdarroch Castle, 42
Crofton, 31, 65
Crown Zellerbach, 65

Deer Islands, 121
Della Falls, 114
Delta Hotels, 82, 107, 110
Demers, Bishop Modeste, 67
Denman Island, 31, 59, 60
Department of Highways
  Ferries, 25, 31
Department of Lands, Forests
  and Water Resources, 115,
  127
Department of Travel
  Industry, 25, 50
Departure Bay, 28, 31, 74, 76
Discovery Inn, 81, 82
Discovery Passage, 19, 61, 62,
  64, 84
Dolphins Resort, 81
Dominion Day, 37
Douglas Lake, 114
Drew Harbour, 63
Drinkwater Creek, 114

Duffin Pass, 138
Duffin Cove Cabins, 138
Duncan, 23, 31, 66, 71
Duncan Bay, 65

East Asiatic Company, 108
Effingham Islands, 125, 129
Eliza, Francisco, 17
Elk Falls, 82, 114
Elkhorn, 19
Elkhorn Mountain, 115
Elliott's Cabins, 52
Empress Hotel, 16, 35, 36, 38, 47
Englishman River, 76
Eskimo, 11
Esowista Peninsula, 21, 125, 138
Esperanza, 33
Esperanza Inlet, 107
Esquimalt, 35
Esquimalt & Nanaimo Railway, 23
Estevan Point, 107
Executive House, 35

Fairy Lake, 52
Fanny Bay, 76
Father Charles Channel, 138
Felice's Ristorante, 40
Fidalgo island, 27
Fike, Captain Stan, 88
Fillongley Provincial Park, 60
Floral Restaurant, 49
Florencia (Wreck) Bay, 129
Flores Island, 134
Forbidden Plateau, 19, 78, 113-115
Fort San Miguel, 104
Fort Street, 45
Francisco Point, 61, 62
Franklin Range, 19
Franklin River, 119
Fraser River Delta, 27
French Creek Marina, 76
Friendly Cove, 33, 103, 105, 123
Front Street, 74
Fuca, Juan de, 18, 99
Fulford Harbour, 31

Gabriola Island, 20, 31, 59
Gabriola Sands Marine Park, 59
Galiano Island, 20, 31, 54, 58, 59
Galiano Lodge, 58
Galiano Rod and Gun Club, 58
Ganges Bay, 57
Gay Nineties, 41
George Inn, 76
George Road, 35

Georgia Strait, 16, 59, 75
Gibson Marine Park, 134
Golden Hinde, 19, 115
Gold River, 23, 33, 65, 82, 85, 95, 99, 108, 110, 113
Gold River Chalet, 82
Goldstream, 35
Gordon River, 131
Government House, 42
Government Street, 35, 45
Gowland Harbour, 62
Graham Island, 97
Granite Bay, 61
Gray Line, 47
Great Central Lake, 77, 114
Green Door, 119
Green Logging, 33
Green Point, 134
Grice Bay, 129
Gulf Islands, 19, 20, 36
Gulf Islands Services, 31

Haida Indians, 43, 97
Haida Inn, 81
Harbour House, 57
Harmac, 65
Haro Strait, 53
Hecate Strait, 97
Heriot Bay, 31, 62, 63
Heriot Bay Inn, 63
Heritage Court, 40
Hernandez, Juan Josef Perez, 101
Hesquiat Indians, 101, 129
Highway No. 4, 117, 131
Highway No. 14, 52
Highway No. 17, 41
Highway No. 28, 109, 113, 114
Historical Sites and Monuments Board of Canada, 105
HMS Discovery, 101
HMS Resolution, 101
Holberg, 93
Hornby Island, 31, 59, 60
Hornby Island Lodge, 60
Horne Lake, 76
Horseshoe Bay, 26, 28, 31
Hot Springs Cove, 134
Hudson's Bay Company, 53, 74

Imperial Eagle, 124
Imperial Eagle Channel, 123
Indian Bay, 129
Indians, 34, 42, 43, 45, 46, 61, 67, 69, 70, 78, 85, 92, 101, 104, 129, 136
Inner Harbour, 26, 35, 42, 47
Inside Passage, 28, 86, 88
Island Hall Hotel, 77
Island Highway, 21, 28, 43, 66, 75, 79, 86, 93
Island Highway 1-A, 35

Island Princess, 86, 88-92
Island Weavers, 45
Ivy Green Provincial Park, 73

James Bay, 34
Jervis Island, 16, 17
Johnson Street, 45
Johnstone Strait, 20, 21, 32, 61, 86
Juan de Fuca Strait, 22, 26, 50, 51

Kelsey Bay, 21, 28, 32, 82, 86, 88
Kendrick Arm, 33
Kennedy Lake, 129, 133
Kiernan, Honourable W. K., 131
Kildonan, 32
Kincolith, 97
Kitimat, 97
Klemtu, 97
Klitsa Mountains, 22, 133
Koksilah, 43
Koksilah's Canoe Store, 66
Komoux, 78
Kuper Island, 31
Kwakiutl Indians, 43, 92

Labor Day, 27
Lacerte Holdings Ltd., 36
Lady Rose, 33, 76, 124
Ladysmith, 73
Lake Cowichan, 23
Lanz, 93
Lasqueti Island, 16, 32
Law Chambers, 40
Le Coq au Vin, 40
Lee's English Toffee Shop, 45
Life Saving Trail, 50, 124, 125, 128, 129, 131
Little Qualicum Falls, 76
Little River, 28
Little Zeballos, 33
Long Beach, 22, 129, 133, 135
Long Harbour, 31
Lougheed, Norman, 69

Mackay, Dr. John, 123, 124
Mackenzie Lake, 114
MacMillan and Bloedel Company, 65
MacMillan Bloedel private roads, 91
MacMillan nature park, 21, 117
Madrona Lodge, 58
Malahat, 66
Malahat Drive, 42
Malaspina Galleries, 59
Malaspina Hotel, 74
Malcolm Island, 32, 86, 91
Manson's Landing, 65

140

Maquinna, 101, 103, 123, 129
Maquinna Park, 134
Maritime Museum (Victoria), 42
Maritime Museum (Tofino), 136
Masset, 97
Matilda Inlet, 134
Mayne Inn, 57
Mayne Island, 31, 57, 58
McPherson's Steak House, 41
Meares, Captain John, 103
Memorial Day, 27
Mill Bay, 32
Miracle Beach, 79
Mitlenatch Island Provincial Park, 85
Money's Pool, 119
Montague Harbour Marine Park, 58, 59
Moovah Bay, 33
Moi●n Lake, 82
Motel Row, 35
Mouat Provincial Park, 57
Mount Albert Edward, 19, 114, 115
Mount Arrowsmith, 117
Mount Baker, 31
Mount Becher, 114
Mount Colonel Foster, 114
Muchalat Arm, 107
Muchalat Inlet, 22, 33, 85, 99, 105, 108
Mud Bay, 76
MV Catherine Graham, 31
MV Coho, 26
MV Comox Queen, 28
MV Cortes Queen, 31
MV Ethel Hunter, 31
MV Island Princess, 32
MV Lady Rose, 32, 121, 131
MV Lasqueti Queen, 32
MV Marabell, 36
MV Quadra Queen II, 31
MV Sointula Queen, 32
MV Texada Queen, 31
M.V. Uchuck III, 33, 85, 105, 109
MV Westwood, 31
Myra Creek, 114
Myra Falls, 113

Nahmint, 32
Nahmint River, 119
Nanaimo, 21, 28, 31, 43, 59, 61, 69, 74
Nanaimo Harbour, 74-75
Nanaimo Lakes, 74
Nanoose Bay, 76
Neuroutsos Inlet, 82
Newcastle Island, 59, 74
Nimpkish, 110
Nimpkish Hotel, 92

Nimpkish Lake, 110
Nimpkish River, 90, 112
Nimpkish Valley, 110, 112
Nitinat Lake, 75
Nootka, 43
Nootka Court, 40
Nootka Sound, 22, 33, 85, 99, 101, 104, 105, 108
Nootka Sound Service Limited, 32, 33
North Cascades, 20
Northland Navigation, 97
Northland Prince, 97
North Pender Island, 31
Nutshell, 41

Oak Bay, 38
Oak Bay Beach Hotel, 35
Oak Bay Marina, 39
Ocean Air Limited, 131
Ocean Falls, 97
Old Bailey, 41
Olde England Inn, 35-36
Old Stone Church, 67
Olympic Mountains, 19
Olympic Peninsula, 35
Opitisaht, 136
Orient Stage Lines, 131
Orlebar Point, 59
Otter Bay, 31
Otter Cave Lodge, 57
Owen Point, 131

Pachena, 125
Pachena Point, 131
Pachena Point Lighthouse, 127
Pacific Ocean, 19
Pacific Rim National Park, 22, 75, 125, 129, 131, 137
Pacific Western Airlines, 25, 107, 131
Painter's Lodge, 81-82
Park Branch, Department of Recreation and Conservation, 115
Parksville, 21, 32, 76, 77, 117
Parliament Archives, 38
Pender Islands, 57
Petroglyph Park, Nanaimo, 62
Plumber Harbour, 33
Point Cox, 129
Polar Bear Swim, 75
Port Alberni, 21, 22, 23, 32, 65, 95, 117, 119, 124, 127, 131
Port Alberni Highway, No. 4, 77
Port Alice, 65, 82, 90, 95
Port Angeles, 26, 27, 35
Port Hardy, 21, 23, 25, 86, 90, 97
Port Hardy Forest Development Road, 91
Portland Point, 129

Port McNeill, 32, 97
Port Renfrew, 21, 22, 50, 52, 124, 125, 127
Port San Juan, 50, 124, 131
Port Simpson, 97
Powell River, 26, 28, 32
Prince Rupert, 26, 28, 36, 86, 97
Princess Maquinna, 95
Princess Marguerite, 26-27
Princess Norah, 95
Protection Island Swim, 75
Provincial Hwy. No. 4, 22
Provincial Hwy. No. 14, 22
Provincial Highway No. 19, 21
Provincial Hwy. No. 28, 22
Provincial Museum, 42
Provincial Parks, 25
Puget Sound, 16

Quadra Island, 20, 31, 61, 62, 75, 81
Quadra, Juan Francisco de Bodega y, 61, 101
Qualicum Beach, 76
Qualicum Beach Chamber of Commerce, 76
Qualicum River, 76
Quamichans, 69
Quathiaski Cove, 31, 61, 81
Quatsino Chalet, 82
Quatsino Sound, 21, 65, 82, 90
Queen Charlotte City, 97
Queen Charlotte Islands, 97
Queen Charlotte Sound, 93
Queen Charlotte Straits, 20, 32, 86
Queenie, 39
Queen of Prince Rupert, 28, 86, 87, 93

Radar Beaches, 129
"Radar Hill," 137
Ralph River, 114
Rathtrevor Beach Provincial Park, 77
Rayonier of Canada, Ltd., 65, 91
Rebecca Spit, 62, 63
Redford Motor Inn, 119
Resolution Cove, 101
Ripple Rock Lookout, 85
River Jordan, 22
Rivers Inlet, 64
Rondeaults, Father, 67
Ronning farm, 93
Ross, Ian, 48
Route Sixteen, 28
Royal London Wax Museum, 42
Royal Victoria Yacht Club, 39
Rumble Beach, 82
Russian River, 108

141

Saanich Inlet, 32, 66
Saanich Peninsula, 27, 35, 47, 69
Sabine Channel, 16
Salishan Resort, 58
Salmon River, 86
Salter, Captain John, 103
Salt Spring Island, 31, 53, 54, 57
Sand Point, 33
San Juan Inlet, 51
San Juan Islands, 20, 27
San Josef Bay, 93
San Josef Valley, 93
Sarita, 32
Sartine, 93
Saturna Island, 20, 31
Sayward, 86
Schoen Lake, 112
School of Music, 42
Schooner Cove, 75, 129, 134
Schwartz Bay, 41
Seabreeze Guest Farm, 60
Sealand, 38, 39
Sea Lion Rocks, 135
Seattle, 26, 27
Seymour Narrows, 85, 86
Shawnigan Lake, 22, 52
Shingle Spit Resort, 60
Ship's Inn, 91
Shoreline Motor Inn, 76
Sidney, 27
Silva Bay Resort, Ltd., 59
Skeena Prince, 97
Sointula, 32, 86, 91
Somass River, 119
Somenos Lake, 71
Songhees, 69
Sooke, 127
Sooke Basin, 52
Sooke Formation, 51
Sooke Harbour, 75
Sooke Harbour House, 52
Spider Lake, 76
Springwater Lodge, 57
Sproat Lake, 22, 75, 119, 133
Sproat Lake Road, 119
S.S. Princess Mary, 41
Stamp Falls Provincial Campground, 119
Stamp river, 119
Strait of Georgia, 53, 63
Strait of Juan de Fuca, 34, 35
Strathcona Park Lodge, 115

Strathcona Provincial Park, 22, 62, 78, 85, 108, 113, 114
Stuart Channel, 73
Stubbs Island, 138
Sturdies Bay, 31, 58
Sunken Gardens, 14
Sunshine Coast, 28
Surf Lodge, 59
Surf Motor Hotel, 35
Sutil Channel, 62, 63
Swartz Bay, 27, 31
Swiss Chalet, 41
Sydney Inlet, 134

Tahsis, 23, 33, 82, 107, 109
Tahsis Chalet, 82
Tahsis Inlet, 107, 108
Tahsis Inn, 107
Tahsis Narrows, 109
Tahsis River, 108
Taku Resort, 63
Tartan Shop, The, 45
Taylor Bay Lodge, 59
Texada Bay, 32
Texada Island, 17
Thetis Island, 31
Thunderbird Park, 42
"Tidal Waters Sport Fishing Guide," 64
Timber Lodge, 119
Tlupana Arm, 107
Tlupana River, 108
Toba Inlet, 63
Tod Inlet, 47
Tofino, 21, 22, 125, 129, 131, 134, 136-138
Tofino Inlet, 129
Tourist Bureau, 35
Trans-Canada No. 1, 21, 22, 32
Trevor Channel, 123
Triangle, 93
Trincomali Channel, 58
Trounce Alley, 40
Tsawwassen, 26, 27, 31
"Tweed Curtain," 39
Tyee C'ub, 82, 84
Tyee Spit, 82
Tyee Plaza, 61
Tyee Village, 119
Tzouhalem Road, 67

Ucluelet, 21, 22, 32, 76, 121, 123, 125, 129, 131, 136, 137
Ucluelet Inlet, 129

Undersea Gardens, 42
Upper Campbell Lake, 115

Valdes, 20
Valhalla Campsite, 58
Vancouver, Captain George, 85
Vancouver Island Coach Lines, 23, 25, 90, 110
Vanlene, 121
Vernon, 110
Vernon Lake, 26, 112
Vesuvius Bay, 31
Victoria, 11, 19, 34, 43, 45, 127
Victoria Day, 37
Victoria Golf Club, 39
Victoria Harbour, 35
Victoria Peak, 19, 86
Victoria, Queen, 38
Victoria Symphony, 49
Vienna Dirndl Shop, 45
Village Bay, 31
Village Square, 40

Washington State Ferries, 27
Welburn, Gerald, 71
West Coast Boatel, 137
West Coast Trail, 124
Western Mines, 114
Westview, 31
Whaletown, 31
Whiffen Spit, 52
White River, 86
Wickaninnish, 101
Wickaninnish Bay, 129, 137
Wickaninnish Beach, 129
Wickaninnish Inn, 137
Wig & Dickie, 41
William Lake, 93
Wilson Inn, 41
Wi'son Motor Inn. 35
Winter Harbour, 23
Woss, 110, 112
Woss Lake, 111
Wya Point, 129

Yaculta, 61
Yellow Point, 73
Yel'ow Point Lodge, 73
Youbou, 22
Young, Captain Esson, 85, 109
Yuquot, 99, 104, 123

Zeballos, 19, 33, 107

142

$1.95 EACH—WESTERN TRAVEL BOOKS FROM WARD RITCHIE PRESS

Trips for the Day, Week-end or Longer

ALL BOOKS COMPLETE WITH MANY PHOTOGRAPHS AND MAPS

QUANTITY   TOTAL

☐ **BACKYARD TREASURE HUNTING** $ _____

☐ **BAJA CALIFORNIA:** Vanished Missions, Lost Treasures, Strange
   Stories True and Tall $ _____

☐ **BICYCLE TOURING IN LOS ANGELES** $ _____

☐ **EXPLORING BIG SUR, CARMEL AND MONTEREY** $ _____

☐ **EXPLORING CALIFORNIA BYWAYS, #1** From Kings Canyon to the
   Mexican Border $ _____

☐ **EXPLORING CALIFORNIA BYWAYS, #2** In and Around Los Angeles $ _____

☐ **EXPLORING CALIFORNIA BYWAYS, #3** Desert Country $ _____

☐ **EXPLORING CALIFORNIA BYWAYS, #4** Mountain Country $ _____

☐ **EXPLORING CALIFORNIA BYWAYS, #5** Historic Sites of California $ _____

☐ **EXPLORING CALIFORNIA BYWAYS, #6** Owens Valley $ _____

☐ **EXPLORING CALIFORNIA BYWAYS, #7** An Historical Sketchbook $ _____

☐ **EXPLORING CALIFORNIA FOLKLORE** $ _____

☐ **EXPLORING THE SANTA BARBARA COUNTRY** $ _____

☐ **EXPLORING SMALL TOWNS, No. 1** $ _____

☐ **GREAT BIKE TOURS IN NORTHERN CALIFORNIA** $ _____

☐ **GUIDEBOOK TO THE DELTA COUNTRY OF CENTRAL CALIFORNIA** $ _____

☐ **GUIDEBOOK TO THE COLORADO DESERT OF CALIFORNIA** $ _____

☐ **GUIDEBOOK TO THE FEATHER RIVER COUNTRY** $ _____

☐ **GUIDEBOOK TO THE LAKE TAHOE COUNTRY, VOL. I.** Echo Summit,
   Squaw Valley and the California Shore $ _____

☐ **GUIDEBOOK TO THE LAKE TAHOE COUNTRY, VOL. II.** Alpine County,
   Donner-Truckee, and the Nevada Shore $ _____

☐ **GUIDEBOOK TO LAS VEGAS** $ _____

☐ **GUIDEBOOK TO THE MOJAVE DESERT OF CALIFORNIA,** Including Death
   Valley, Joshua Tree National Monument, and the Antelope Valley $ _____

[SEE MORE BOOKS AND ORDER FORM ON OTHER SIDE]